The Best
Women's Stage Monologues
of 2005

edited by D. L. Lepidus

MONOLOGUE AUDITION SERIES

A SMITH AND KRAUS BOOK

Published by Smith and Kraus, Inc.
177 Lyme Road, Hanover, NH 03755
www.SmithKraus.com

First Edition: January 2006
10 9 8 7 6 5 4 3 2 1

Cover illustration by Lisa Goldfinger
Cover design by Julia Hill Gignoux

The Monologue Audition Series
ISSN 1067-134X
ISBN 1-57525-428-X

NOTE: These monologues are intended to be used for audition and class study; permission is not required to use the material for those purposes. However, if there is a paid performance of any of the monologues included in this book, please refer to the Rights and Permissions pages 98–101 to locate the source that can grant permission for public performance.

Contents

The Best
Women's Stage Monologues
of 2005

Foreword

The monologues in this book have been culled from the best plays published or produced during the 2004–2005 theatrical season. All are from published, readily available plays (see the Rights and Permissions pages at the back of the book for publisher information).

Many of the monologues herein are by playwrights of considerable reputation, such as Michael Weller, Charles Busch, Israel Horovitz, Kathleen Tolan, Stephen Adly Guirgis, and Paula Vogel. Others are by future stars, such as Winter Miller, Sheila Callaghan, Allison Moore, Sarah Ruhl, and Lisa D'Amour. Most are monologues by characters under forty, although there are a few great geezer monologues, such as the one from *The Outrageous Adventures of Sheldon & Mrs. Levine.* I made a conscientious effort this year to find some great monologues that will be of particular interest to teen actors, such as the ones from *Jewish Girlz, Cavedweller, Common Ground, Elephant, Eloise & Ray,* and *Squats.*

In short, this is the best darn monologue book I could put together. I know you will find in it that perfect piece for your audition or class use; but if you want some more options, check out Smith and Kraus' other fine monologue collections.

Many thanks to the agents, publishers, and authors who have allowed me to include these wonderful pieces in this book.

— *D. L. Lepidus*

THE BEARD OF AVON
Amy Freed

Comic
Anne Hathaway, thirties

> The Beard of Avon *is a wild farce about the Shakespearean authorship controversy. Here, Mrs. Shakespeare has come to London, curious about her husband's life there, disguising herself as a "woman of loose morals." This is direct address to the audience.*

ANNE: Ooooh, LONDON! Well, life is certainly strange. 'Twould never be believed in a FICTION that my own husband might not penetrate my disguise —. Oooh, what adventures have I had! Once arrived in Colin's rags, I went to see my cousin Lucy, a bawd about town. She took me in and thrilling to my device, outfitted me in her own sluttish fashion. Such THINGS she has! That push you IN where you go OUT, and puff you OUT where you don't actually. Paints as white as poison and rouge as red as roses! Cheek patches, corsets, chokers and gloves . . . shoes that make you taller than your own dumpy self — for once in my life I'm slender! No wonder why my husband loves the theater! I never want to go home again — and just look at this hair! Had I only been a man, I might have been an . . . actress. *(Pause.)*
    Well. Thus trimmed and decked I sought out my own love — and contrived to meet him just after the matinee. (*Titus Andronicus* — now THAT be entertainment!) Well. He knew me not as his wife, but thought me a wicked whore. He took me to his rooms, and we've scarcely been apart for a week. I've been just AWFUL to him. It's been WONDERFUL. Well, he himself hath taught me cruel inconstancy, since faithful kindness prompted him to flee.

BRIDEWELL
Charles Evered

Comic
Kristen, twenty, a student, obsessed with her weight

Kristen commiserates with her sorority sisters about men.

KRISTEN: Look, just be glad you're not me. Maybe I do have a little issue with food. I remember when a certain someone RIPPED MY HEART OUT. It was my total low point. I was going to those Overeaters Anonymous meetings with my mother — which is kind of ironic, because she's the person who used to shove food in my face all the time anyway. It's kind of like going to a Serial Killer's Anonymous meeting and having Ted Bundy drive you there. So, this certain someone DUMPS me and as my mother is driving us home it's like; what do ya know, she just happens to stop at a Rite Aid and out she comes with a ten-pound box of candy and all I remember after that was seeing our twenty pudgy little fingers pulling and twisting and gouging out the candies and me just shoving them into my mouth and that's when I got this great idea; "I won't eat them," I thought. I'll just chew them. If I chew them without swallowing, then I never will have eaten them at all. And all of this will have been nothing but a bad dream. So I put like fourteen of them in my mouth and I just *chomped*, but without swallowing, feeling all the chocolaty juices sliding down my throat and my brain flooding with endorphins and after about eight minutes I hacked out this huge ball of nougat and caramel and deftly wrapped it up in a napkin and calmly put it on the dashboard and repeated the process over and over until all the candy was gone. Would that qualify as a "food issue" would you say?

CAVEDWELLER
Kate Moira Ryan

Comic
Dede, a teenager

> *On the morning of her sister Amanda's wedding, Dede, who's a*
> *bridesmaid, smokes a joint with her sister and tells her about a*
> *recent job interview she had.*

DEDE: Walked right in to get lunch — Skittles, Coke and a pack of Men-
thol 100s, police tape everywhere, body in a bag, one of the clerks
pulled off his 7-Eleven shirt and threw it at the manager's feet. He
said, "I ain't working blood" and walked out. I picked up the shirt
and I looked the manager dead straight in the eye and said, "I got an
eye for trouble. Very little that people can do, that I wouldn't know
how to figure. I could be good." He looks at me like I'm crazy. "Good
at what?" He asks me. "This place, this job. I've been stealing quar-
ters from that Muscular Dystrophy sign since I was so high. This is
something I know a little about."
    Damn straight. "I can handle this job." I tell him. He looks me
over and says, "Girl, you are tiny. And somebody got shot here this
afternoon. Died." I don't waiver my stare and I say, "I ain't going to
get shot. I know how to handle myself, and there's not much that
can stop me when I make up my mind. No, I ain't no two-hundred-
pound ex-jock, but I can get things done. I could run this place like
you cannot imagine." He hands me the shirt, and I say, "Tell me the
secret behind the papaya slushie." Here, don't believe what they tell
you about this stuff. It's like a bottle of beer but you don't get bloated
or nothing. Makes you a little hungry, though, that's it. I've been getting this stuff from Billy Tucker. He's been growing it next to his
Daddy's sarsaparilla. *(Beat.)* You look like a Quaker in that dress.

CAVEDWELLER
Kate Moira Ryan

Comic
Dede, a teenager

> *Dede, a wild and rebellious teenage girl, is in jail for having shot a guy. Here, she is talking to her mother Delia, who has come to visit.*

DEDE: Fucking waitress that served me beer and chicken wings, and him DOING HER LIKE THAT! Saying he loves me and then the two of them together. I knew it was a trick all along. She wasn't just there to pick up the keys to Biscuit World. She wasn't just there doing him a favor. Oh, no. I went back to apologize and then I saw her at the door. Looking at him like he was one of *People* magazine's Most Handsome Men Ever. The gun was under the seat of my car, the one I got after Billy Tucker scared me. I don't even remember going for it. Seemed like I was watching them and then I was shooting. "You want to marry me?" I shouted and shot him. If Nolan loved me right, this would have never happened. If Nolan loved me right, he would have left things alone. I told him to let it alone. You think about how I felt, believing him, trusting him, letting myself love him and him to do me like that? I trusted him. I trusted him.

CAVEDWELLER
Kate Moira Ryan

Dramatic
Delia, forty

Delia is sitting in a diner talking to her daughter, Cissy, about a pivotal moment in her life, which occurred when she was eleven years old and was deserted by her parents, left to live with her nasty grandfather.

DELIA: *(Delia takes a long drag from her cigarette and puts it out.)* It was 1959, the summer I was eleven. We were getting ready to go on a trip. We were going to drive over to Fort Jackson — the whole family — to pick up my Uncle Luke, my daddy's brother who was finishing up basic training. It was going to take a day to drive there and a day to drive back, two hot days in the summer heat in a car without AC. I was set to go. We were saying good-bye to Grandaddy Byrd when he discovered a litter of puppies under the tractor. I was thinking about the heat and the puppies. Thinking about how I'd be wedged between my older brothers driving through two states without a breath of air. So I told my daddy that I wanted to stay with Grandaddy Byrd. Boys couldn't believe that I would give up a chance to sleep in an air-conditioned motel and miss seeing the soldier's parade. They couldn't believe it. My daddy picked me up and hugged me tight. My mama kissed my forehead. I cupped my hands against her pregnant belly like I had been doing in the last month whenever I said good-bye or good night to my mama. *(Pause.)*

Four days passed, then six. We didn't hear a thing. After a week Grandaddy Byrd went to Jackson to help my Uncle Luke search. He came back confused and angry. Nothing was known, nothing was discovered. Then Grandaddy drowned the puppies, lifted them one at a time in his big knuckled hands and thrust them under the water in an old washtub. He laid them out side by side to bake in the sun.

I bit the inside of my cheeks so I would not scream. *(Pause.)* They did find the car just before Christmas at a dealer's lot in Savannah. Uncle Luke came home for three days. Christmas morning I found him passed out drunk in the living room. I looked into his opened mouth. He was silent. Not a word about my parents, my brothers. Grandaddy Byrd was silent. I felt that silence creep through my body. I balled up my fists and hit my uncle as hard as I could. Grandaddy Byrd came out and lifted me up off him. I began to kick him until he dropped me. I remember them staring at me. I heard this wail, this shrieking. It was me. I cursed them all. Uncle Luke and Grandaddy, but also my mama and my daddy and whoever had stolen them. I would have cursed God if I could have confronted him. I've been cursing ever since. That pretty voice everyone thought they heard, that was me cursing. That was my anger, my grief.

THE CLEAN HOUSE
Sarah Ruhl

Seriocomic
Matilde, twenties

> *Matilde, a Brazilian woman, is in America working as a cleaning woman for a wealthy couple. In this direct address to the audience, she talks about how her parents died.*

MATILDE: The story of my parents is this. It was said that my father was the funniest man in his village. He did not marry until he was sixty-three because he did not want to marry a woman who was not funny. He said he would wait until he met his match in wit.

And then one day he met my mother. He used to say: Your mother — and he would take a long pause — *(Matilde takes a long pause.)* — is funnier than I am. We have never been apart since the day we met, because I always wanted to know the next joke.

My mother and father did not look into each other's eyes. They laughed like hyenas. Even when they made love they laughed like hyenas. My mother was old for a mother. She refused many proposals. It would kill her, she said, to have to spend her days laughing at jokes that were not funny.

(Pause.)

I wear black because I am in mourning. My mother died last year. Have you ever heard the expression "I almost died laughing?" Well that's what she did. The doctors couldn't explain it. They argued, they said she choked on her own spit, but they don't really know. She was laughing at one of my father's jokes. A joke he took one year to make up, for the anniversary of their marriage. When my mother died laughing, my father shot himself. And so I came here, to clean this house.

COBRA NECK
Keith Josef Adkins

Dramatic
Woman, twenties, Black

> *The daughter of a local parish is haunted by her mother's coura-*
> *geous acts of truth telling. When she attends a Tupperware party and*
> *comes face-to-face with the scorn of the local community, she decides*
> *to scratch away her mother's memory for good — literally. This is*
> *the second half of a longer monologue.*

WOMAN: Why did I have to be her daughter? The one woman in town who goes to a Tupperware party and opinionates that we're living on a toxic dump in this town, which is doubling our risk for cancer, get out or die, she pleaded. Watches their jaws drop to the floor, and then check for extra appendages before laughing. Then she ditches this death trap to live on a tanker with a musician from Belize. And what about the backlash those opinionated opinions would have on small-minded folks in a small-minded town who wouldn't believe the sky was falling if it dropped over their heads. They laugh at you, Momma. They put your picture up at the Pic-n-Sav, and somebody drew a mustache over your lips. They don't like know-it-alls and opinionaters. Only truth-telling somebody they want is the one nailed to a cross.

(Calmly:) So they just keep pointing out my arms, feet, and saying they're just like yours, praying some truth will come bubbling up from my inside, through my long snake neck, and spill on their shoes. I say, no, I'm one of you, I'm not like her. But they don't care. They just want a reason to post my picture up at the Pic-n-Sav, and draw a mustache over my lips. *(Then:)* And, oh, how I wish.

I do try. To opinionate. *(Takes a breath, then:)* Your weaved hair is aiding in the rise of self-hatred. But it won't leave the brain, Momma, connect to the voice and fall from my mouth. I try to telepathy it to 'em.

(She tries to "telepathy" the opinion to the partygoers.)
See. Nothing.

It's because I wasn't born to speak something great, and educate a town strutting around with extra nipples. And even if I did say something great, it would fall flat, and not-a one jaw would drop to the floor. At least what you said made them think for one split second. That's why I gotta keep making it harder for them to recognize me in you. 'Cause I don't have the gumption for that honor. Yet.

(She pulls a pair of scissors from her sock, then takes the scissors to her neck. And as she begins scarring, lights go down.)

COMMON GROUND
Brendon Votipka

Dramatic
Teenager, either male or female

This monologue, "White Crayon," from Common Ground *by Brendon Votipka, was written for a young person in high school. It may be used by an actor of any gender or age.*

TEENAGER: I've been trying very hard to put into words the way I'm feeling right now. But I'm drawing a blank. I feel blank. "Blank" is almost something, but I fear it may be nothing. Nothing is an awful feeling. It's the absence of feeling. I don't feel nothing. Nothing is not what I feel. I feel something. Definitely something. I don't feel the absence of feeling, but I think I may feel the absence of color. Until I got out my art supplies from kindergarten, I couldn't decide what it was. Then, It hit me.

I feel like a white crayon. No, I don't. I am a white crayon. Exactly. I am completely and totally a white crayon. I guess I always identified with the white crayon. The thing is, the white crayon just sits in the box. You following me? I mean, I know that all the colors sit in the same box. Back in grade school, when you bought your school supplies at the beginning of a school year you could be sure that every color would be present. But while you can be sure they're all there, does it matter that every color is in the box? Does it matter if you have a white crayon? No.

The others colors get so much more action. Of course they get more action. Take a color like green. I wish I was green. Green is used in so many pictures, so often. How frequently does a kid use green. Pretty frequently. It gets a lot of action. Red is the same way. You use red for an apple, or a heart, or lips. Purple can be grapes, or flowers, or a sunset. Yellow, blue, brown, black, pink, any color, you name it!

People use those colors all the time. A kid uses every crayon in the box.

Except white. No one ever picks up the white crayon. It sits in its box, completely sharpened and ready to go, but it's destined to remain in the stupid box. No one needs it. It has no use. I know, I know, "people use the white crayon sometimes." But rarely. Rarely. And besides, the white crayon is the crayon no one cares if they break. If they snap in two, no big deal. It's not like it's necessary for survival. No one needs a white crayon.

THE CRAZY TIME
Sam Bobrick

Comic
Kate, about fifty

Kate is talking to Miles, her ex-husband, telling him off for carrying on with a much younger woman.

KATE: Please, please Miles. You don't have to make any polite excuses. You wanted to get laid by a young chick. It's understandable. What fifty-six-year-old man doesn't?

Too bad. Between you and me, it's not always easy having to talk to young people. Anyway, Miles, I now can understand your little misguided transgression perfectly. Older men are attracted to younger women. It's as simple as that. It's not a new phenomenon. It's been that way since the beginning of time. But trust me, Miles, I don't care what breakthroughs medical science makes, an older man will never get the sexual satisfaction from a younger woman that an older woman will get from a younger man. And best of all, when we have sex, I don't have to wait a half hour for a pill to work.

Yes, life without you Miles didn't turn out so badly after all. Thanks to your walking out on me, I now have an exciting life too. Maybe it will last forever and then maybe it won't. Who knows? But while I want to be with Dirk, and he wants to be with me, *honey*, all older men can kiss my ass.

CUTRS!
Allison Moore

Comic

Andrea Anderson, could be any age

Andrea is urging us to join her organization, which seeks to exhort "consumers" to spend more money by shopping till they drop.

ANDREA: We all feel badly for the people who have been laid off. Let's agree on that. People like my friend, "Ted."

"Ted," who is a hard worker and loving family man who can't find a job. His wife is working overtime, his daughter's mouth is a train wreck, but they can't afford their mortgage let alone braces. And it's *hard*. But do you really think you're going to *help* Ted by *not buying* a new beach tote?

By clutching your money in a tight, guilty fist instead of opening a charge account at IKEA? Do you?

Well then, let me tell you about another number. It's the most important number of all. It's called the Consumer Confidence Index.

It tells businesses and manufacturers if we are ready to get out there and BUY what they are SELLING.

If we are going to *spend* —

Or if we are going to *sit,* in our houses, in the dark, while overstock gets dusty on the shelves and distributors and manufacturers go *out of business,* taking *thousands* of jobs with them, *all because we FEEL BADLY for people like "TED"?* Let me tell you something: if everyone refinanced their houses and went to the *mall, we wouldn't need charity! They'd all have jobs!*

CUTRS is issuing a call! A call to *revolution!* A call to banish unemployment by banishing this debilitating guilt! Take every credit card they offer you! Fuck the voting booth and get your ass to the ATM! This is war! Your country needs you! *Spend! Spend!! Spend!!!*

(Andrea stands, her fist raised in a power gesture.)

My name is Andrea Anderson, and I am the founder of CUTRS: the Committee United to Radicalize Shopping. I was honored as a megastar by the Mall of America for spending more than a hundred thousand dollars there in 2003.

Your country needs you. Join us.

DARK RIVER
Alexa Romanes

Dramatic
Liza, cockney streetwalker

Liza is a streetwalker in Victorian London, here talking to Frank, her brother, a "mudlark," about her life on the streets.

LIZA: I don't know why I've come back 'ere, after the last time. You're my brother, Frank, I care about you. I worry about you. I think about the river all the time. I just know that you'll either freeze to death or catch a fever. I can buy you clothes. I can give you a home. My circumstances 'ave changed. I've got a regular gentleman. A real toff. 'E gives me enough every week to rent my own place. It's not far away — Pinchin Street in Whitechapel. You'd like it. It's real cozy — and it's all mine. I don't 'ave to share . . . Oh, don't be like this, Frank. This is my chance. And yours, too.

Well, what would you do, Annie? You know what it's like. There's hundreds of us — thousands, probably, with a bad start in life. Dad kicked me and Frank out on the street when Frank was only six. I took care of 'im as best I could, and I'm still trying. Maybe the wrong way — I don't know . . . it's funny. I see people all around so much worse off than me. Last night, for instance. I was in a pub near the Opera House with my gentleman, and this old woman came in, begging. Well, she was trying to sell flowers, but she only 'ad a few wilted bunches of violets. She shuffled in, wheezing like a pair of old bellows. Her face was all twisted, like she'd 'ad a stroke or something, and you should 'ave seen 'er hands. She could hardly hold the flowers. So I says to my gentleman, "Don't take the poor old woman's flowers, just give 'er the money." So 'e does, and she were that grateful she 'ad tears in her eyes, and then she kissed my hand — imagine it — and then she mumbled, "May God forgive you, my dear." *(Pause.)* She were grateful — but at the same time, she pitied me.

DEN OF THIEVES
Stephen Adly Guirgis

Comic
Boochie, twenties

Boochie is an "exotic dancer." She is tied to a chair in a room with three other people, also tied to chairs. Perhaps, they are going to be executed. Here, she explains why in her case this would be a great shame.

BOOCHIE: Thank you. *(She clears her throat.)* Society would suffer if I die for many multiples of reasons. Number one: As a exotic dancer, I bring smiles to the faces of many sad lonely mens, and sometimes womens too if they into that. Number three: I am extremely fly — as you definitely noticed — maybe in the top ten of flyest women in the city, and if they serious about keeping New York beautiful then they gotta need me around, right? . . . I'm also a sexual surrogate, which means I fuck for educationalism, which is important to society since I teach mens to fuck better, and God knows womankind could use more mens who fuck better — right, Maggie? I provide that. I also teach fellatios to the womens which I'm sure most mens could appreciate . . . Number eight: I believe in charity. When I get famous, I plan on donating a lot of money to the Ronald McDonald House so sick children of all ages could always eat McDonald's for free, so even when they die, they'll die happy. Oh, also I belong to the A.S.P.C.A. . . . . *(Pause.)* One more thing, which, I don't even know why I'm saying this, but, I got abused a lot as a child, people. A lot. And I ain't sayin' that for you to feel sorry for me, even though I wouldn't mind if you did feel sorry so I could be one of the survivors, but, the point of this is that everyone in my family called me "garbage can," including my mother, which I think dat ain't very nice, but also I think is very false 'cuz I ain't no fuckin' garbage can! And even though I gots lots and lots of talents which make me definitely a big bargain for the society, even if I didn't have *any* of those amazing skills and dreams which I, like, process — even if I *was* a garbage can — which I'm not — I'd still be valuable 'cuz where you gonna put your garbage if you don't got no can? Someone's gotta be that can, right? So, for all these ideals and many more, I feel I am a valuable ass to society and many, many peoples of all the five boroughs, and maybe even the world, would have their lives be more messed up if I wasn't around to be around . . . Dass it. Thank you.

DIE! MOMMY! DIE!

Charles Busch

Comic
Barbara, forties to fifties

> *Barbara is the "twin sister" of Angela Arden, a faded singer in this*
> *spoof of 60s movie thrillers. She is of course played by the same actor*
> *who plays Angela (in the original production, the inimitable Mr.*
> *Busch). Here she is talking to a "gentleman" at the bar where she's*
> *planted herself tonight.*

BARBARA: *(To a gentleman at the bar.)* Yes, I'd love another cocktail. I'll
order them. *(To the bartender.)* Jimmy, two Bourbon Manhattans,
please. *(To the gentleman.)* Are you sure you don't want a fresh one?
The ice is all melted out . . . Why do you keep staring at me? Oh I
know. You're wondering what a big star like Angela Arden could pos-
sibly be doing in a dive like this. I shall dispel the mystery. I'm her
untalented twin sister, Barbara, Barbara Arden . . . That's not why
you were looking? You know, you're very sweet.
  (Barbara mimes talking in a phone booth.)
  Mother, I'm calling from City Hall. I've just been married. I'm
Mrs. Jack Murphy and oh, he's a darling boy. I know you'll
really . . . What, Mother? Angela's concert tour broke all records?
That's terribly exciting. I just wanted to . . . Hello? Jack, for the first
time in my life, I'm not jealous of Angela. I have a wonderful husband and a perfect baby. I'm so happy and proud that we've never
had to borrow even a cent from my sister. I'm in a cave filled with
little white monkeys. They're crawling everywhere. All over me. Look,
there's a submarine floating this way. I believe the captain is Mrs.
Dean Martin. No, it's not a submarine at all. It's a car. Be careful.
Get out of the way. It's going so fast. Get out of the way? *(To Angela.)* Angela, after the car accident, Jack and the baby dying, I've
tried to get along by myself but I can't seem to find any work. I'm

broke, flat broke, with no prospects. I suppose I should tell you, I'm a jailbird. I've done time. Three years in San Quentin. It all started not long after the car crash. I took a position as Assistant secretary to the comptroller of the Department of Sanitation. However, very quickly I could smell that something was rotten. Your honor, I was framed, framed like a high school diploma! I'm innocent! Why won't anyone believe me.

After three years and a private audience with the Lieutenant Governor, I was sprung for good behavior. And well, here I am. Frankly, Angela, I'm at your mercy. *(Barbara turns into Angela.)* So you show up on my doorstep a convicted felon, a failure and expect a handout. Do I have much choice? It certainly wouldn't look good for Angela Arden Sussman to turn away her own sister. *(As Barbara.)* Oh Angela, you're so very fortunate. A brilliant career. Lovely home. And Sol couldn't be a more wonderful man and the children. That beautiful little girl and Lance, so precious. *(As Angela.)* Don't be such a sap, Barbara. My life is perfectly hideous. I'm tired of singing for my supper. Am I nothing but a voice? And my marriage? You have no idea what kind of man Sol really is. And the children? Well, Edie's all right, I guess, but there's something very wrong with Lance. Thank Heavens, you've taken an interest. Just looking at the child makes me ill. And it's all my fault. Nobody cares about me. If I dropped dead tonight, no one would moan. No one would mourn. *(Barbara, to herself.)* If my sister died. If my sister died, I should be free. I could *be* Angela. A better star, a better wife, a better mother. No, no, don't think that way. You mustn't. You mustn't covet your sister's house, your sister's husband, your sister's songs, your sister's son.

(To herself.) The house is empty. The children are with the governess. Put the pills into Angela's vodka. She's so drunk, she'll never know. How many will she need? Are these enough? Then exchange clothes. Lie her down on my bed. It's so simple.

ELEPHANT
Margie Stokley

Seriocomic
Michelle, late teens

*Michelle's therapist, Tad, is trying to get her to deal with the loss of
her brother, Jay. Here, Michelle, not quite ready to reveal the de-
tails of Jay's accident, tells the group about how witnessing someone
else's loss gave her hope.*

MICHELLE: He died twenty minutes from our house . . . don't bother lean-
ing in Tad, that's about all you're gonna get. Stay tuned.

I know this girl . . . Danielle . . . her best friend Cheryl was killed
last year. They weren't family. They chose to spend the years
together and that's cool. I didn't know Cheryl well. We weren't really friendly. She sat in front of me in Social Studies. But after she
died Danielle looked different. I looked at her differently . . . everyone did. Kinda like the way you are all looking at me now. You feel
sorry for me. You can't help it. I get it. But when Danielle came to
my brother's wake — I was excited — for real excited! Excited that
finally there was someone in the fucking room who had been broken too. And it gave me hope.

(Exaggerated.) HOPE.

Hope that someday I'll walk into a room and the sign on my
forehead reading lost, broken, and angry will be gone. I am so tired
of selling my life stories to people I don't know.

The good news is he can't die twice. Once you're dead . . . you're
dead! Game over. You go to rest knowing you'll never be sad again.
You'll never be told *"no."* You will never have someone you know die.
You'll never be sent to an institution and forced to take someone
named *Tad* seriously. Sounds like heaven to me. Sign me up! Now
let's recap — My brother's dead. My family can't start over. I'm here.
My life sucks. Next.

ELEPHANT
Margie Stokley

Seriocomic
Michelle, late teens

> *Michelle's brother, Jay, a marine in his twenties, has recently died in a car accident, leaving behind his parents, Henry and Kathleen, Michelle, and his pregnant girlfriend, Ellen. Separately, they deal with their loss, and together, they find ways to move forward. Michelle is in a hospital with an apparently ineffectual therapist named Tad, obsessively over-applying makeup and lashing out at the world as she battles her sadness. Here, she is introducing herself at group therapy.*

MICHELLE: Hi. My name is Michelle.

(She does a crazy gesture and noise that somehow mocks suicide.)
Just kidding

No, really — thrilled to be here. What do you want to know? What do you want me to say . . .

(Silence.)

Oh wait, that's right. This is not a conversation — it's a session. This is my time to share, with *complete strangers,* how I feel . . . Well, I feel like talking about trees. How do you feel about them? Wait.

Please, don't speak . . . let me. My fascination *stems* from this one tree.

(She silently mouths stems *again to emphasize the irony.)*
Rough crowd.

(A pause.)

Well, it's gigantic and right outside my bedroom window. Some nights I feel like it wants in. Wants in to my perfect pink and white striped room. My room is perfect, not because it's everything I want. It's just perfectly planned, the pillows, the balloon shades, the pictures, the bed, the window seat, my stuffed animals. I have even more animals under my bed. I have guilt about suffocating them . . . I feel, it doesn't matter. They don't match.

(A pause.)

They really don't. Well, it can't fall now because I just predicted it. What you think is going to happen — never does. It's a relief. You can't know it all. I just feel like in *my movie* that's what will happen. There'll be a huge thunderstorm with lightning, my tree will explode, and I'll be crushed. I can see myself split in half. I don't want to be surrounded by all those people who would need to be there if I got crushed. I am over groups. No offense.

ELOISE & RAY
Stephanie Fleischmann

Dramatic
Eloise, sixteen

> *Eloise, sixteen, in the act of running away from her boyfriend Roy's empty house, collapses in her spot on the curb, where she will end up sitting for three days and nights. On video, we see a condensed time recap of those three days and three nights as she sits by the side of the road. We watch her face weather as each day elapses.*

ELOISE: On the first night, I learned to see in the dark.

On the first day after the first night the sun beat down. It burned right through me, dried me out to nothing, blinding my see-in-the-dark eyes, so I saw light where there was shadow. I saw through layers of days.

On the second night, I heard what wasn't there.

I heard words spoken behind my back a hundred miles away.

On the second day after the second night the rain beat down and washed what the sun had dried away. Water drummin', gutter river rushin'. I heard voices in the pounding. My mother — ? I heard my — No. No, it was The Actress. And Jed? No. It wasn't Jed. Who I heard that day was Ray.

On the third night, I learned to smell moving shapes in the dark with my nose. I learned to sniff out creatures without hearing or seeing. I learned to tell a lizard from a lynx just by its smell.

ELOISE & RAY
Stephanie Fleischmann

Dramatic
Eloise, sixteen

ELOISE: I said to Rosanna. "Him and me, we — He devirginized me. Yesterday. I am now de." And she said, "Congratulations. From this moment on, in honor of this, I will call you DeVee."
And I said, "Not around my daddy, you won't."
"That's right," she said. "He would KILL you if he found out. But MY lips are zipped."
And then she looked at me and she looked at me for the longest time, and I said, "What are you staring at?"
And she said, "I'm trying to see if you look different."
"Do I?" I said. "Do I look different.?"
And she said, "No. You look like Eloise. You look like you always did. Do you feel like her?"
"Her?" I said.
"Eloise," she said. "Same old same old."
"But the same old same old feels different every day," I said. See-through.
"You know what I mean," she said.
And so I told her: "I do. I feel different."
Glow in the dark.
"I feel like I am his and he is mine and he will never leave me. He will never let me go."
"Well, that's a cliché if I ever heard one," said Rosanna.
"But I do," I said, "I feel different. I feel a changing — I am the me that was always meant to be."
"You be careful," said Rosanna. "That's a dangerous business."
"You wanna know how I really feel?" I said.
"I feel like an oyster. All this time I been an oyster, and I never even knew it. All this time takin' in sand and takin' in sand and it's been working on me, working inside me to make this — This pearl. Only it took him to pry me to open and pick it out."

FABULATION
Lynn Nottage

Seriocomic
Undine, thirties, Black

Undine had a successful P.R. firm until her husband absconded with all her money. Here, she is talking to her friend Allison as repo men are dismantling her office.

UNDINE: No one seems troubled by the actual charges against me. No, the crime isn't being a criminal, it's being broke. It's apparently against the law to be a poor black woman in New York City.

(Whispered.) They auctioned off my furniture; it was like a feeding frenzy, people I knew bidding on my possessions waving little flags and purchasing bits and pieces of my life for a bargain.

At some point I thought they were actually going to put me up on the block and sell me to the highest bidder. And in a flash I thought, "Thank God I got my teeth done last year." "Look at them teeth, she got a fine set of teeth y'all." How naïve, foolish of me to assume that I was worthy of some comfort and good fortune, a better chance. They give you a taste, "How ya like it?" then promptly take it away. "Oh, I'm sorry we've reached our quota of Negroes in the privileged class, unfortunately we're bumping you down to working class." Working. I'm not even working. I think I'm officially part of the underclass. Penniless. I've returned to my original Negro state, karmic retribution for feeling a bit too pleased with my life.

FABULATION
Lynn Nottage

Dramatic
Inmate #2, could be any age, Black

> *We are in an encounter group for drug addicts, who have been re-*
> *quired by court order to attend. Here, one of the women talks about*
> *how she has come to be here.*

INMATE #2: Shit, all I was doing was buying formula for my cousin
Leticia's baby over on Myrtle avenue, right? And this dude, was you
know, all up in my panties with his eyes. Right? On my shit like he
my man. "You don't know me brother," I told him. But he gonna
get all pimp on me, like I's his bitch. Big fat Jay-Z acting muthafucka. He think he all that 'cause he drivin' a Range Rover in my
neighborhood. That don't impress me. Show me a pay stub, Brother.
Show me a college diploma. But this dude is gonna step to my face.
I told him, put your hands on me and see what happens.

   Why you think I'm here? I showed the muthafucka the point
of my heel and the ball of my fist. I told him, "I ain't your 'ho." "I
work from 9-5 at Metrotech, my man, don't you look at me like a
'ho, don't you disrespect me like a video 'ho." Now, he gonna think
twice 'fore he place a hand on another woman. Believe it. People think
they know your history 'cause of what you wearing. Well guess what?
I introduced him to Gloria Steinem with the back of my mutha-
fucking hand.

FABULATION
Lynn Nottage

Dramatic
Undine, thirties, Black

> *Undine has really been through hell. Once the owner of a success-*
> *ful P.R. firm, she lost everything when her husband absconded with*
> *all her money. She has been arrested for trying to buy heroin — not*
> *for herself but for her addicted grandmother, and has been ordered*
> *by a judge to attend an encounter group for drug addicts. Here, she*
> *starts out talking to Guy, an addict in the group, but expands her*
> *confessional to include everyone, finishing up with Guy, who might*
> *be the only person who can redeem her.*

UNDINE: I've never heard anyone say I'm happy and actually feel it. People around me say it automatically in response to how are you doing?
But when you say it, I'm looking at you, I believe you actually mean
it. And I find that reassuring.
    Because mostly I feel rage.
    (Undine realizes the addicts are eavesdropping and finds herself
including them in her confessional.)
    Anger, which I guess is a variation of rage and sometimes it gives
way to panic, which in my case is also a variation of rage. I think it's
safe to say that I have explored the full range of rage. And it has been
with me for so long, that it's comforting. I'm trying to move beyond
it, sometimes I even think I have, but mostly I'm not a very good
human being. Sometimes I'm less than human, I know this, but I
can't control it. I killed my family.
    (A collective gasp.)
    Yes, I killed them. It was on the day of my college
graduation. Dartmouth. My family drove 267 miles in a rented mini
van, loaded with friends and relatives eager to witness my ceremony.
They were incredibly proud, and why not? I was the first person in

the family to graduate from college. They came *en masse*, dressed in their Alexander's best. Loud, overly eager, lugging picnic baskets filled with fragrant ghetto food . . . let's just say their enthusiasm overwhelmed me. But I didn't mind, no, I didn't mind until I overheard a group of my friends making crass unkind comments about my family. They wondered aloud who belonged to *those* people. It was me. I should have said so. I should have said that my mother took an extra shift so I could have a new coat every year. My father sent me ten dollars every week, his lotto money. But instead I locked myself in my dorm room and refused to come out to greet them. And I decided on that day, that I was Undine Barnes, who bore no relationship to those people. I told everyone my family died in a fire, and I came to accept it as true. It was true for years. Understand, Sharona had to die in a fire in order for Undine to live. At least that's what I thought. What I did was awful, and I'm so sorry. And Guy, you are such a good decent man. And I wouldn't blame you if you walked away right now. But I don't want you to. I feel completely safe with you.

I am not yet divorced, I'm being investigated by the FBI, I'm carrying the child of another man and I'm not really a junkie.

Are you still happy?

And you're not medicated?

FREE GIFT
Israel Horovitz

Dramatic
Heather, mid-twenties, Black

Heather has come to Roselle's home to sell her life insurance. The women begin talking about their lives.

HEATHER: I remember going to a funeral of a old friend's father . . . in Brooklyn, when I was maybe twenty. Stephanie. Stephanie was somebody I went to first grade with . . . The father had been married before, a long time before he'd married the mother. We knew there was another daughter somewhere, but, we didn't know that the father had been keeping up with her, with this other daughter . . . keeping in touch . . . being a kind of daddy, on some level. At the funeral, the casket was, you know, open. The father was dolled up in a blue suit and red tie and his skin was kind of this weird gray/green color. He was a really dark-skinned man, but you wouldn't've known this from lookin' at him. Well, the church was packed and the choir was into it, when alls'a' sudden this woman about thirty years old starts yellin' "That's not my daddy! He's not my daddy!" . . . It was this other daughter. And we all start thinkin' "He really doesn't look like Stephanie's daddy! . . . Maybe they switched him with some other body by mistake?" It was amazing, 'cause everybody had this very same thought at the very same time. People got the giggles, I swear to God! *(Heather laughs.)* That's the thing about being alive, isn't it? . . . You always want to laugh. No matter what, there's always, like, that energy. When you stop wanting to laugh, you're dead.

HANDLER
Robert Schenkkan

Dramatic
Terri, forties

> *Terri is a middle-aged woman in the rural South. Terri is standing
> at the grave site of her daughter, speaking to her husband, Geordi,
> who is fresh out of prison for what we will eventually learn is the
> accidental death of their child.*

TERRI: I get over when I can and pull them weeds. Usta come all the time
but they always grow back. Even when I dig 'em out by the roots.
Sister Alice said I ought to use weed killer but that don'ts seem right,
somehow. Poison. Don't know why it should matter but it does. And
sometimes I bring flowers. We get to keep what we find in the rooms
we clean, long as it ain't real valuable. That's the rule anyway. But if
somebody left a big ole sack of money I can't see myself turning that
in to the front desk. Know what I mean? You find some strange
things, I tell you what. The usual stuff, underwear and liquor bot-
tles and condoms but you also find some strange things. Cheryl found
a leg, once. Honest to goodness. A plastic leg. Had a black shoe on
it. Loafer. Little tassels.

(Shakes her head.)

Anyways, sometimes, people order flowers up to their rooms.
Anniversaries and suchlike, I guess. Special occasions. I don't know
why they leave'm. I wouldn't. I mean, even if you didn't want to car-
ry'em back wet in the car, you could always dry'em, you know? Or
press'em inna book. Keepsakes. Remembrance. Some people set up
vases of plastic flowers out here but that always seems so tacky to
me. Plastic. Be puttin' up pink flamingos and daisy wheels next.
Gravel's the new thing. White, shiny gravel. Can you believe that?
Dump it by the truckload. Cain't nothing push up through that,

believe you me. And if your . . . your dearly departed looks like a garden path or the bottom of a fish tank, well, that's just too bad, inn't? Me, I'd rather pull them weeds on my hands and knees.

(Terri falls to the ground and begins yanking fiercely at the weeds.)

HATE MAIL
Kira Obolensky and Bill Corbett

Seriocomic
Dahlia, twenties to thirties

> *Dahlia is speaking out loud a letter she has written to Preston, a man who had entered her life through a nasty complaint letter sent to her place of employment. Here, she has just learned that he has purchased some self-portrait photographs.*

DAHLIA: Hello, or should I say What the Hell?!

I write to ask you a question, not to resurrect the sputtering dialogue of months ago.

Some background information: My exhibition was not the hoped-for critical success. Apparently, depicting the unclothed female body amid the urban pastoral of the 20th century is more "suited to a Calvin Klein ad." (This from one of my ex-lovers, who I have discovered is just another snob underneath all that Comme des Garcons.) My circle of pseudo-feminist/intellectual/"friends" have accused me of creating "pornography that objectifies the female form for male/capitalist consumption." *Exactly!* . . . I would say, if for one second I was given the opportunity to defend myself! It's political, you morons! The body depicted is my own: the artist's body, displayed, revealed, to be tragically consumed by market forces as a tourist might covet a trinket.

Which brings me to my main point. Despite the overwhelmingly negative response, every single photograph in the exhibition has been purchased. The gallery dealer will tell me only that the anonymous collector is "a gentleman from the Midwest."

The idea that you might own 12 photographs of my naked body is very alarming to me. Did you purchase my photographs? And if you did (a thought that makes every hair on my body stand at attention) WHY?

HAZZARD COUNTY
(That's What It Means to Have a Duke Heart)
Allison Moore

Comic
Jessica, twenty

> *Jessica, a Canadian woman, is obsessed with the TV series* The
> Dukes of Hazzard. *This is direct address to the audience.*

JESSICA: You know they're taking it off the air? Well, I mean again, you
know, off the cable. The Bastards! I signed the petition about a million times. But they have to bring it back. I mean, we're too devoted,
the fans? And there a lot more Dukes of Hazzard fans than regular
people think, even here. Some people try to make it sound like it's
weird that I'm such a huge fan. Like you can only be a fan if you're
from Georgia or something, or really into cars? But any one who looks
at my site figures out that my heart is true, you know? Doesn't matter if I'm from Manitoba, I have a Duke heart. That's why they keep
coming back, to my Hazzard online. Well, unless they're creeps just
looking for nude pictures of Catherine — and I say Catherine, because Daisy would never pose nude, she's a virgin? And besides, Uncle
Jesse would kick her ass if she did. And when he was done, Bo and
Luke would take turns kicking her ass, too. But mostly Luke, because Bo'd be too hurt to kick her ass. He'd be too hurt that she would
sell her self and dishonor the family like that. And Luke would see
how hurt Bo was by it, and that'd make Luke even madder because
he can't stand to see Bo hurt. And then they'd have to fight everyone who had the picture? Go out and track every asshole bastard
down and punch him, and tear the picture up, or burn it. And Bo,
Bo would be burning the very last picture, that they got off this real
bad guy who was gonna post it online. And Bo would be about to
light it, the very last negative of Daisy, and the bad guy would trip
him. And Bo drops the torch and the whole place catches on fire.
And the bad guy grabs the negative and makes a break for it. And

Luke is about to follow him but he looks and sees that Bo's on fire. So Luke grabs a blanket and wraps him in it, before they jump through the flames. And Bo's coughing from the smoke, and Luke would say "Are you all right, Cos?" And Bo would say, "Don't worry about me, did he get the negative?" And Luke would say, "Not if we have anything to say about it." And they'd jump in the General just as the bad guy is pulling out. He's desperate to get away with the negative because he's a sick bastard who wants to see Daisy brought down to a whore. And Bo and Luke realize they could send him heading straight for Mill Creek where the bridge is out. So they put out a fake call on the CB, saying they've decided to run one last shipment of moonshine.

And back in town, Roscoe and Boss Hogg are listening to the CB monitor, while Boss eats a huge pile of ribs. And he won't share, because he's a Hogg. But Roscoe sneaks a rib from the plate, and just as he's about to take a bite: They hear the Dukes' plan on the CB.

And Boss, he smacks Roscoe and snatches a rib, and Roscoe runs to the squad, licking his fingers and cursing them Duke Boys. And he hightails it to the turnoff just in time to see the porno fucker — who Roscoe thinks is Luke, driving the shine. And the guy sees Roscoe and freaks, and turns down the creek bridge. But before he has time to even think about all the beating off he's gonna do with that picture, he drives through the barricades, airborne, and lands in the creek. His filthy negative is ruined, and Roscoe arrests him for stalking. Because it turns out, Daisy was doing some wash down by the creek, and her clothes got all wet, and she had to take them off for a minute to let them dry in the sun. And while she was waiting that rapist was spying on her with a super powerful lens. And everybody apologizes to Daisy, Uncle Jesse and Bo, and Luke especially, because he can be kind of a jerk sometimes because he's the oldest and he was in the Marines. But he knew in his heart that Daisy would NOT pose for pictures like that because she is pure. And Daisy forgives him, because she knows if Bo and Luke weren't around, she could have been raped and tortured and chained in a closet like a dog. But they look out for each other because they're kin. They're all each other has in the world. That is what it means to have a Duke heart.

JEWISH GIRLZ
Elizabeth Swados

Seriocomic
Nessa, teens

> Jewish Girlz *is a musical about a group of Jewish teenaged girls at a summer camp. They sit around the campfire, sing songs, and tell stories about their lives. This is one of them.*

NESSA: I can relate to great heroines. My Bat Mitzvah was OK. I had the portion about the golden calf. It's very dramatic — all that hedonism and idol worship. The Israelites lost faith waiting for Moses to come down from the mountain. Once when I was four my mother was caught in traffic and came forty-five minutes later to pick me up from Hebrew school. My mom wouldn't let me have a cell phone. I was sure she was gone forever. That she was dead or had run away with some other girl who was going to be her daughter. By the time she finally pulled up I had gone through the five stages of mourning and was onto my shaky recovery. I was almost disappointed that she was still alive. In this way I explain to you the story of the golden calf and the state of mind of the Israelites. I danced with my father at the party. I danced with my cousin too. No — I didn't dance with any boys. I hung out. You don't dance with boys to some adult jazz orchestra. *(Sings.)* "Strangers in the night — two lonely people — we were strangers in the night." I think if I could've had the Bat Mitzvah of my dreams it would be much more like a Broadway musical. My hair short and blonde and in spikes or — like Meg Ryan's. Only I'm dressed in rags — sexy rags. And I'm approaching with fire inside — a stone podium (it's ancient times) the people are dancing and worshipping the golden calf. But there I am singing my Bat Mitzvah portion, which is actually a ballad of faith and endurance — like "When You Walk Through a Storm" from *Carousel.* And the entire millions of Israelites including my mother and father and stupid younger brother are falling to their knees — they are so completely moved. They realize I'm right. Never worship false idols. Trust in Moses. Whatever — And here, under a spotlight, with the stringed orchestra, I transform into an angel. I'm lifted over the audience (like they do in *Peter Pan*) and I glow — I actually glow. I'm Celine Dion with wings. Only Jewish. That's how a Bat Mitzvah should be. That's how life should be I just hope we don't have to get undressed in front of each other. I'd die if anyone saw me in mid development. Neither here or there — that's my body.

JEWISH GIRLZ
Elizabeth Swados

Dramatic
Rebecca, teens

> Jewish Girlz *is a musical about a group of Jewish teenaged girls at a summer camp. They sit around the campfire, sing songs, and tell stories about their lives. This is one of them.*

REBECCA: Richard is his name — no one calls him Rick or Dick — he's Richard. And he's tall and he dresses in good jeans and a blue T-shirt that says OK OK on it and he's tall, you know, really tall and he actually has dimples and this dark hair that's smooth like the side of a brown waterfall. And Randi says to me — I think Richard likes you and I tell her I've known him forever. We've been to all these parties though I've never really danced with him. And once I saw him outside the mall at night and he had been drinking beer. And he never said hi Rosie or anything and I heard him and his friends laugh and I thought they were laughing at me — typical suburban teenage paranoia. So he comes up to me at the mall and Randi sort of pushes me forward — obnoxious girlfriend style and he says "Hi Rosie, you wanna go for a ride?" And I go, "OK, Richard," and we walk away from Randi and Dora and I know what they're thinking because I'm thinking it too. And I'm thinking he might drive me by the ball field or behind the small strip of stores on Elmwood Street and I'm saying to myself, "Am I gonna do it? Am I gonna make out with him? Am I gonna French kiss with him? Let him feel me up?" So I'm a little nervous, you know, because I'm hoping we can talk some more than ahem, mm yuh, and so on and he's kind of a friend so I'm wary of changing directions. But if he's romantic about it — just some talk and a long kiss — not wet — that would be a good start. So we kind of float out to the parking lot and it's all tar like a kind of dark moon and it's the middle of the day so the sun has stolen the breeze. And we're walking and he says, "Hey Rosie I see you got your belly button pierced." And I nod affirmatively and he says cool. So we get into his really expensive smooth and shiny mustang and he beeps it with his key chain and all that and I'm in my seat and I'm looking at the speedometer and the gas gauge and the buttons for the heat and the wipers and the CD player and the digital clock and it's all so lined up and perfect and glowing. "Hey," I say, "This is like some major B52 bomber," not knowing what I'm talking about and he's looking straight ahead, not saying anything and then I feel his long hand cup around my neck. And like an unexpected fall down the stairs, he's pushed my head into his lap and he's just holding me there keeping me down like a wrestler who has no opponent and I feel him pulling down his zipper and he says, "Do it Rosie. Give me a blow job." I'm quiet now wondering why people do it at all if it's so uncomfortable. And I'm measuring whether this puts me in the hierarchy of the popular kids at school or would I be a slut. Where does this act fit into my coolness? And he says, "Do it Rosie. Give me a blow job. Everybody does it. It's safe. You won't get pregnant, Rosie. Blow me, blow me." And I get this feeling again like if I get into one more event where my life is measured by a do or don't I'll kill myself and this time it won't be a rehearsal. Because what I do adds up to how I'm thought of and how I'm thought of is who I am. "Do it Rosie," Richard says to me. He and my parents sometimes ate at the club together. Not like close friends, but enjoyable company. Richard and I would walk around the golf course and we were just friends, but I still was waiting for him to kiss me. I'm always waiting for someone to kiss me.

JEWISH GIRLZ
Elizabeth Swados

Dramatic
Amanda, teens

> Jewish Girlz *is a musical about a group of Jewish teenaged girls at* *a summer camp. They sit around the campfire, sing songs, and tell* *stories about their lives. This is one of them.*

AMANDA: Here I am at my sacred altar — the toilet. We just had pizza and pizza has mozzarella cheese, which is 346 calories. Tomato sauce doesn't amount to much, but I'd better add it in so let's give it 65 calories. So that makes that one slice comes to 534 calories, which is way over my allotment for a meal. I figure if I throw up the pizza, I'll be back to zero or maybe 100 calories will stay inside me if I don't get everything out. I'm in here and this is a private ritual simply for me. It's a cleaning of the system and purification. It pisses me off that all the teen magazines and talk shows are talking about it as if it was flossing. Or doing abs. Like it's that popular. It's like when all those pot smoking lost hippies take up Hasidism in Israel all of a sudden. It's a phony religion. I've been doing this since I can't remember when. It's part of me. You'll never see me on any talk show. This is a secret, my moment with the Goddesses of Beauty. This is what I have to do. I live for it. Literally it's why I live. No one told me that — but you just know when you're called.

KALIGHAT

Paul Knox

Dramatic
Sydney, late twenties

> *Sydney came to Kalighat to explore the possibility that she has a calling to join the Missionaries of Charity as a nun. Although it has its rewards, she finds the work grueling and at times horrifying. Another difficulty is that she finds herself confused by her attraction to Peter. When she finally hears her answer, she returns to Kalighat to try to make Peter understand her decision.*

SYDNEY: I took a train up to Darjeeling, where Mother got her calling. Guess I thought if it could happen to her, it could happen to me. You should go. So beautiful. Surrounded by the white cliffs of the Himalayas. Watch the sunrise over Mount Everest. I'd go for walks through the hillside tea plantations. All by myself, so quiet, for hours each day just walking, praying, listening. Trying to hear something, you know? Some answer. Can I do this work forever? Did I have the strength? But I didn't hear anything. No mystical voice. One day I just sat down on a rock, looked down the mountain into the river running through the valley and cried. I don't know how long I was there, just lost track. Suddenly it got very dark and began to pour down, sheets. So much rain I couldn't see in front of me. I tried to run, but the mud started washing away from under my feet, so I grabbed onto a tree. I was drenched and so scared I'd fall down. It only lasted a few minutes, then it turned into a very gentle rain. I looked out across the mountains, the clouds separated and the sun began to shine through, and a rainbow appeared across the entire valley. My heart was beating and I stared out over that loveliness and that question was just spinning around in my head. And it dawned on me, suddenly it made so much sense. The voice I was trying to hear was the question itself. It had been there all the time. And I knew the only way to answer it was to try.

THE LAST DAYS OF JUDAS ISCARIOT
Stephen Adly Guirgis

Dramatic
Henrietta Iscariot, forties to fifties, but could be any age

The case of Judas has been reopened, in a trial in Purgatory, and various people are testifying as to the merits of the case, which is about whether Judas is villain, victim, or hero. Henrietta is Judas' mother.

HENRIETTA: No parent should have to bury a child . . . No mother should have to bury a son. Mothers are not meant to bury sons. It is not in the natural order of things.

I buried my son. In a potter's field. In a field of Blood. In empty, acrid silence. There was no funeral. There were no mourners. His friends all absent. His father dead. His sisters refusing to attend. I discovered his body alone, I dug his grave alone, I placed him in a hole, and covered him with dirt and rock alone. I was not able to finish burying him before sundown, and I'm not sure if that affected his fate . . .

I begrudge God none of this. I do not curse him or bemoan my lot. And though my heart keeps beating only to keep breaking — I do not question why.

I remember the morning my son was born as if it was yesterday. The moment the midwife placed him in my arms, I was infused with a love beyond all measure and understanding. I remember holding my son, and looking over at my own mother and saying; "Now I understand why the Sun comes up at day and the stars come out at night. I understand why rain falls gently. Now I understand mother" . . .

I loved my son every day of his life, and I will love him ferociously long after I've stopped breathing. I am a simple woman. I am not bright or learn-ed. I do not read. I do not write. My opinions are not solicited. My voice is not important . . . On the day of my son's birth I was infused with a love beyond measure and understanding . . . The world tells me that God is in heaven and that my son is in Hell. I tell the world the one true thing I know: If my son is in Hell, then there is no Heaven — because if my son sits in hell, *there is no God.*

THE LAST DAYS OF JUDAS ISCARIOT

Stephen Adly Guirgis

Comic

Saint Monica, could be any age, but in the New York production was played by a woman in her twenties

Saint Monica is a very sassy woman, who could be any age, or any race. In "real life" she was the mother of St. Augustine. We are in the After Life, and there has been a petition to reopen the case of Judas Iscariot. Saint Monica is very much in support of this petition.

SAINT MONICA: Hey, y'all. Welcome to my world. . . . So this is the part of the story, where, if it wasn't for me, there wouldn't be no more parts to the fuckin' story, OK? My name is MONICA — better known to you mere mortals as SAINT Monica. Yeah, dass right, SAINT — as in "better not don't get up in *my* grill 'cuz I'll mess your shit up 'cuz I'm a Saint and I got mad saintly "connects," OK? You ever drove down Santa Monica Boulevard? You ever ate some sushis down the Santa Monica Pier? Well, dass *my* boulevard and *my* pier, and dass all I gotta say about that — word to the wise, word is most definitely B-O-N-D bond . . . Anyways, (lemme catch my breaf), Anyways, Up in Heaven, a lotta peoples don't wanna hang with me 'cuz they say I'm a "Nag." It's true. And you know what I say about that? I say; "Fuck them bitches," 'cuz — you know what — I *am* a Nag, and if I wasn't a nag, I wouldn't never made it to be no Saint, and the church wouldn't a had no Father of the Church named Saint Augustine — 'cuz I birthed the mothahfuckah, raised him and when he started messin' up, like, all the time and constantly, I nagged God's ass to save him! I nagged and nagged and nagged and nagged 'till God got so tired of my shit that he did save my son, and my son — Saint Augustine — he stopped bangin'

43

whores and sippin' on some wine and he became learn-ed, so fuckin learn-ed that he's known as one of the Fathers of the Church, and you could look that shit up! Go ahead, look it up right now, I'll wait! . . . Dass right: "Father Up In This Mothahfuckah!" "Father of the Church" — got a plaque and everything! So if I hadn't been a Nag, All a Y'all niggas woulda been a bastard church, so, sip on dat, bitches! . . . Anyways, (lemme catch my breaf), OK: As a result of my reputation of having God's ear, a lotta mothahfuckahs pray to me — I have three full-time assistants just to sift through it all. Long story short, I was axed to look into the case of Judas Iscariot by this Irish Gypsy lawyer bitch in Purgatory named Cunningham. She wanted me to do some naggin' to God on Judas' behalf, and, quite frankly, I was impressed by *her* nagging abilities — 'cuz that bitch nagged my ass day and night for forty days . . . But I don't nag for juss any anybody, and I definitely don't nag for no mothahfuckah I don't know, so, I went down to check out Judas for my own self —
(And now she is with Judas.)
(To audience.)
He looked fuckin' retarded, he wouldn't talk or nuthin. He didn't seem to hear me, and I'm not someone who has a problem expressing myself. I figured he was fakin', so I did this:
(To Judas.)
Yo, Judas! . . . Judas! . . . Yo, You Deaf,
mothahfuckah? . . . . Judas, yo! . . .
(To audience.)
I smacked the bitch around a little
(Monica slaps, kicks, shoves.)
Yo Helen Keller! Yo, wake up! . . . Don't front — I know you could hear me . . .
(To audience.)
Then I started snappin' on his ass:
(To Judas.)
Yo, Judas, you got chance for thirty pieces of Silver, mothah-fuckah?! . . . Yo, Judas, how much you pay for that haircut? . . . thirty pieces of silver?! Yo Judas, why you so "hung" up? C'mon, let's "hang" out. C'mon, bitch, go out on a "limb"! You want a "olive"? C'mon

mothahfuckah, have a "olive." Wanna go to the "Olive Garden" restaurant? Day got good "Olive Oil" there . . . Ah-aight, fine, come on, Judas, whaddya say you an me go down to the bar and — betray some mothahfuckahs! Whaddya say?! I know you like betraying! What's up, you ain't in the mood to betray today?! Ah-aight, mothahfuckah, we can just "hang"?! Get it? Hang?! Get it?! Do you get it?! . . . Wassamatter?! Hungry?! How 'bout some supper?! You want some supper, mothahfuckah?! C'mon, one last supper, whaddya say?!

(To audience.)
I couldn't break him. So I sat down next to him.

(She sits.)
I sat with Judas Iscariot for three days.

(To audience.)
Then, On the night of the third day, sumpthin happened. While I was restin' my vocal chords, I saw sumpthin' unexpected. I saw a single tear fall out Judas eye. Just one. When the tear hit the ground, I saw it was red like a ruby. I looked into his eyes, like this:

(Monica looks into Judas' eyes.)
He couldn't look at me. Or he looked through me. I couldn't tell. His eyes was empty. He barely breathed. He was like a catatonic statue of a former human being. And I detected sadness in him. Paralyzing, immobilizing, overwhelming sadness. His sadness ran through him like a river that had frozen up and died and no one lived there no more. After a while, I didn't know what else to do, so I thought I'd just hold him in my arms for like a minute, warm him up before I left.

(Monica cradles Judas in her arms. Beat.)
I held him in my arms for four days. On the third day, I remembered how Jesus had said that God has the biggest love for the least of his creatures — and Judas was the least-est creature I had ever seen. On the fourth day, Judas dropped another single tear. It was clear-colored this time and it evaporated into the earth on impact. He trembled briefly, then froze up again . . . I had seen enough. I took off my outer garments and left them for him so he could smell something human. I collected my tears in a bucket and poured it on

his face so he could taste the salt. Then I went back home and got on the horn to God. I dialed direct, yo. Some people call it being a Nag, I call it doing my Job. I got a calling, y'all — you should try giving me a shout if ya ever need it, cuz my name is Saint Monica, I'm the mother of Saint Augustine, one of the Fathers of the Church, and ya know what? My ass gets results.

THE LAST DAYS OF JUDAS ISCARIOT
Stephen Adly Guirgis

Dramatic
Cunningham, thirties to forties

> *Cunningham is an attorney who has brought a petition to the court to re-open the case of Judas Iscariot. Here, she is questioning a witness — a fella named Pontius Pilate.*

CUNNINGHAM: You wanna know what I really think, Mr. Pilate? I think this whole story about you hemming and hawing about what to do with Jesus is just a load of made-up crap written by Jewish Christian Evangelists seeking to broaden the appeal of the Jesus story to the Roman Empire. There is nothing that we know about you, Mr. Pilate — absolutely nothing — that suggests for even a second that you would have even a passing hesitation about putting *any* Jew to death — let alone a Revolutionary figure like Jesus who was being proclaimed The Messiah, who had entered the city of Jerusalem to crowds of cheering supporters, and who had the very next day incited a riot at the Temple. You hated your assignment, you hated Judea, and, Mister Pilate, you hated Jews. Hated them. You hated the Jews because they contested you. You hated them because they fought back.

You hated them because they clung to their religious beliefs and were willing to die for them. But most of all, I think you hated them because you knew they were stronger than you. I think that bothered you a great deal. I think, Mister Pilate, that it made you resentful and vengeful and furious. I think it made you feel small and inadequate. I think it gave you skin irritations and nervous tics. I think it kept you up nights and made you count the days until you could return to the safe, bourgeois comfort of Rome. That's what I think.

I think you're hiding behind historical inaccuracies and outright lies, Mister Pilate. I think that you're a liar and a fraud. I think that when Jesus was put before you, you did not see a God or a prophet, you did not see a lunatic or an innocent, you didn't even see a human being. I think, Mr. Pilate, that what you saw before you that morning was just one more Jew, and you didn't hesitate. Why would you? . . . You didn't wash your hands, Pontius Pilate — History did it for you. Isn't that true?

THE LEFT HAND SINGING
Barbara LeBow

Dramatic
Claire, forties

> *Claire is the mother of a college student who has vanished during the Freedom Summer of 1964.*

CLAIRE: Rose Kennedy. Rose Kennedy, I hate you. Your noble suffering. You have buried three sons to my two. And a daughter. I believe. How bravely you bear it! Standing in fashionable black at one grave after another after another after another. Here, in this place, they tell me about you frequently. Perhaps they think you will be an inspiration for my recovery. Perhaps I don't wish to recover. Some of the photographs, they tape up in my room. On occasion, I am led to a television set and placed before it to watch yet another documentary about your cursed, courageous family; you at the center, the tiny, intrepid monarch, your dyed hair, your frozen face. *(Screaming.)* Why don't you tear your hair out, Rose? *(Pause. Regaining control, then carefully again.)* You glide through your grief like a dancer born for the role. Like you accept your destiny without question, showing up to mourn as required. *(Screaming.)* Why don't you wail like a colored woman, Rose? And throw yourself on the grave? *(Pause. Quietly.)* My oldest son, Jack, had nightmares as a child, when his daddy was overseas in the war. Did your boy? I held him tight and let him sleep with me. Did you comfort your children in your bed, too? Did they comfort you? *(Screaming.)* Did they? *(Quietly.)* You have gotten used to losing your children, Rose? I have not. I will not. I choose not to. I chose not to attend the service for Wesley. Not to see his father drop what's left of him in the ground, next to what's left of his brother.

THE LONG CHRISTMAS RIDE HOME
Paula Vogel

Dramatic
Claire, thirties

> *For most of the play, the actress playing Claire plays her as a child.*
> *Here, we are twenty-five years in the future. She is trying to get into*
> *her apartment, which she shares with her girlfriend Naomi.*

CLAIRE: Naomi? Naomi. Naomi. Naomi. Come on, answer. I saw you go
in. Naomi. Naomi.

Naomi? Naomi? I'm going to play "Jingle Bells" on the buzzer
until you let me in —

"Dashing through the snow; in a one-horse open sleigh — o'er
the fields we go — laughing all the way — Ha! Ha! Ha!"

*(Suddenly the gaiety is gone; Claire slumps for a moment. Then she
steps out onto the street.)*

They won't answer the intercom. That's not a good sign. I know
they're in there. I tracked Naomi all the way from the apartment and
I saw her go in. Ostensibly to study with Betty for tort class.

She's been studying a lot, lately.

As my luck spirals, I keep looking more and more for signs. As
harbingers of fate. On the sidewalk the entire way here I didn't step
on a single crack. So, tonight is the night. The Feast of Stephen.
Tonight. I'm looking for the sign — one way or the other — for what
the future holds. If Naomi looks out the window — if she sees me
down here on the sidewalk — if she stops what she's doing — If, if,
if! . . .

Ah, the floor show is about to begin. Anyone parked in a dark
car or standing on the sidewalk looking up at the second-floor window can see it. Second floor, third window from the left. . . .

Naked lesbian law students. They'll make out like this for a long time, until Betty's law school work ethic pops up, stronger than their libidos: time to crack the books for tort class.

Naomi, I'm down here. I'm watching. Look down here, I'm down here. . . .

Once upon a time, I went through my own golden girl stage. I determined a long time ago that I would never again be a golden girl, but oh I could bed them. I still can't believe that I talked these girls into sleeping with me: tall, blue-eyed, blonde — the difference in height just spurred me on: as they stretched themselves down on the bed, they were a large canvas, and I a young Jackson Pollack, ready to fill every inch.

Naomi, Naomi, down here — I'm down here. . . .

OK; tonight will be the night that Naomi stops; she thinks for a moment, she remembers me and — . . .

And she comes back to me . . . Naomi . . . For God's sake, stop . . .

Oh — oh that's not a good sign. I fear my Naomi has found her golden girl.

(Beat.)

I am so very tired. I still wake on cue every four hours without an alarm; time to give Stephen his AZT. It would be about that time now.

And near the end with Stephen . . . Fantastic pale lavenders and dark maroons ravaged the canvas of his skin until only his hands remained unchanged . . . a young boy's hands . . .

My hands are cold.

(Claire draws out mittens without fingertips and puts them on; she hesitates.)

There should be a word for me. "Cuck-old." Such an ugly sounding word. There should be a word for a female of the species.

I always imagined cuckolds murderous in a red hot rage, but it doesn't feel like that at all. It feels like inside it's snowing . . .

(Claire sits there for a long moment. She reaches under her coat and brings out a revolver. Claire checks the ammunition and snaps the barrel closed.)

If she'd answered the door. If she'd looked down my way . . . If I hadn't lost Naomi. If I'd kept Stephen alive. If If If . . .

THE LONG CHRISTMAS RIDE HOME

Paula Vogel

Dramatic
Rebecca, twenties to thirties

*Rebecca is trying to get into her apartment, which she shares with
Chester.*

REBECCA: Chester, Chester! What are you doin' home? Hey Chester — My
keys aren't working in the lock! Come on down an' let me in, it is fucking freezing frigid. Chester! I'm down here on the street —. . .

When was I going to tell you what? . . .

Did you read my Mail?! . . .

OK. So I'm pregnant. Shit happens. I was gonna tell you when
you got back home — Congratulations! Now let me in the goddamn
door. The mother of your whatever-it-is is freezing to death out
here. . . .

I had a drink with the girls at Toppers! A little Christmas ho ho
ho — I had One little drink!

(To herself.)

An' about five little chasers . . . I'm not keeping it anyway. . . .

What are you calling me? . . .

You always were a son of a bitch with math. So you were out of
town on a business trip three months ago — wait a minute — did
you go through my Diary? Did you? Did You Read My — ?! . . .

OK, OK! The "R" in my Diary stands for Rick. . . .

Chester! Chester! For God's sake — STOP!

Chester — honey — unlock the door, let me in, and I'll pack a
bag. . . .

I don't know where I'm going this time of the night. It's too late
to go to my mother's. Do Not Call My Mother, Chester. She's upset

already this time of year. I mean it. Don't you dare call Mom. I don't want to ruin her Christmas. And forget my bunking in with Claire she thinks the sun shines out your ass . . . I could sleep on the couch tonight. I'll be gone in the morning. . . .

Why? Why? I don't know why! Because . . . because. When you're not here . . . I need to be noticed. . . .

Oh Baby. Don't cry, baby. Come on, Chester, let me in. . . .

You want me to keep the baby? You want us to raise it together — I don't think that's a good idea. . . .

You want me to marry you? . . .

We could call him *Stephen?* Or *Stephanie* if it's a girl!? Don't you dare fucking manipulate me by using my brother! No one is going to replace my brother. Ever! I hate feeling this baby using me like some *host* body — . . .

No! I am not playing nursemaid to children! Great. I'll come by tomorrow when you're at work and pack up — or — no no — Screw it all.

You go boy! I don't care! Just throw out all my shit with the trash — . . .

Oh Screw You, Chester! You son of a bitch — that's . . . pathetic! You change the locks, and now you want to raise his bastard child?! A real man would come down here and slap the crap out of — . . .

— You're warning me! Chester?! You don't have the balls! . . .

"Have yourself a Merry little Christmas . . ."

Shit. You'd think I'd know by now not to leave my Diary lying around . . .

Oh boy. I've got to sleep it off in the back seat of the car . . . where the hell did I park the car . . . blocks and blocks away . . . Christ it's cold. They're sayin' on the radio not to let your dogs and cats out tonight . . . I gotta get off the street . . . I'm not going to think about this right now. Just find the car. I've had practice not thinking about stuff in a room at the Holiday Inn . . . There's so much not to think about . . . you have to not to think about the green paisley of the bedspread . . .

I think I parked down this block . . .

(Rebecca reaches where the car should be.)

Damn . . . This doesn't look familiar. Think, Rebecca. Maybe it's the next block down — Oh, Jesus, I need to lie down. Wish I were at the Holiday Inn. The Comfort Inn, the goddamned Dollar Inn. *(She continues to walk, very haltingly.)*

Turn down the next block —

(She walks some more.)

And who the hell picks out the pattern for their headboards?

(She trails off. Looks around.)

Shit. This isn't right. It's the other way.

(She stumbles on.)

And then you have to concentrate on feeling the weight of his thighs so you won't think about his wife waiting at home, the kids listening for his key in the . . . So many things not to think about . . .

God, Rebecca, you just threw it all away.

(Rebecca stops, completely lost. The wind turns.)

I'm not gonna make it to the car. I've got to sleep. Now . . . Oh look . . .

That snowdrift looks like the cleanest sheets I've ever seen . . . A four-star hotel! Room Service! They've turned down the sheets . . .

(Rebecca lowers herself onto the "drift" and curls up. She removes her scarf and bunches it up to form a pillow. She speaks to her stomach.)

It's funny — It's so cold you can really see your breath, but I don't feel cold at all . . . just very sleepy. We're gonna curl up together, all snug and warm, and . . . just . . . fall . . .

(Rebecca is out cold on the bench.)

MEMORY HOUSE
Kathleen Tolan

Dramatic
Maggie, late thirties to forties

Maggie is trying to cajole her teenaged daughter, Katia, into finishing her college application essay.

MAGGIE: I can't believe I'm baking a pie. I used to be an interesting person. . . .

I've become a caricature. We are required to dumb-down, to become dull, neutral, to allow the child to grow and flourish and assert herself and find her own way, not be in the shadow of her mother's large personality — . . .

We play a role and of course it's reinforced when the child becomes a teenager or even earlier, when we voice an insight or tell a joke or sing a song or anything, really, and the anguish this causes, the rolled eyes and severe chastising that we be put in our place — . . .

And I do understand it, of course I understand it, I, believe it or not, was a daughter — . . .

I too had great contempt for my mother and truthfully she, in retrospect, took it with much more restraint and grace than I am or maybe it was that she is just more repressed, I like to think that's it, but really, I just don't get it because you know, I really am a very cool person. . . .

And I realize this is pathetic. . . .

I'm just saying that we play a role and it may be a necessary role but then we can't remember how to get back.

MEMORY HOUSE
Kathleen Tolan

Dramatic
Katia, eighteen

> *Katia was adopted when she was about nine and brought to this country from Russia. She has been asked to write an essay for a college application about her "memory house," but she's procrastinating, much to the chagrin of her mother, to whom she's delivering this rant.*

KATIA: Well, what do I write? That I'm a victim from a bleeding country? . . .

That I owe my life to the people who took advantage of the tragedy of Russia and ripped me off which was great cuz now I don't have to be a hooker on the streets of Moscow but — oops — now I'm a citizen of the country of bullies? . . .

And all these other countries and people hate us because we're bombing them and fucking with them and I'm the spoils of that. I don't know where to go, what to do — go back to Russia? Why would I do that? Stay here? Why would I do that?

(Beat.)

Meanwhile my friends are all totally freaking out about their fucking stupid test scores and their totally inane application essays and jackass interviews and their parents are flipping out and acting like their kids are trying to kill them, as if their kids are thinking about them at all, this is so totally not about them and they think it is and so they have to deal with debilitating lunatic parents on top of everything else.

(Beat.)

And I'm thinking, don't they get that we're the bad guys? And don't look at me like this is some teenage thing or some psychological thing or like you have to protect me and go along. There are

le getting killed, people dying, this fine countr,
a terrible life is sending soldiers to poor count
ent people. And you know what? If I were tending
, just trying to eke out some way to feed my childre
with the simplicity and the joy and the hardship of the su
morning and the moon at night and just getting the blueber
the truck for the man with the clogged arteries to drive it up to
for your pie, just doing my back-breaking work, and doing my be
and out of the big sky came a bomb that tore up my field and killed
my dear children and my dear wife and my dear friends and neigh-
bors and I had *nothing* and it was because this big rich country
wanted to get some guys they thought might be hiding somewhere
who were lunatics or who were so angry and no one was helping them
and they were so fucking angry that they had strapped a bomb to
their backs and they were willing to explode their lives, to just blow
them up because they were so insane and angry and desperate. How
would I feel? What would be the thing to do?

(Beat.)

I mean, what do I say on these things, what the fuck do I say?

n Tolan

atic

a, eighteen

Katia was adopted when she was about nine and brought to this country from Russia. She has been asked to write an essay for a college application about her "memory house," but she's procrastinating, much to the chagrin of her mother, to whom she's delivering this rant.

KATIA: If there is anything of value — any thought or feeling — why put it in a college essay? Why put little secret pieces of memory in a pitch to fucking guys who couldn't figure out how to have their own lives, leeches who have to suck off our lives, and what about our strange affliction of having to learn more? What about that? . . .

    And what business is it of anybody's, my past, and everybody's assumptions about my past, and putting it into a fucking box to look at and have theories about? And get degrees about. Let's get a degree about my dead mother. Let's write a paper about how I'm a refugee from a broken land. That's my angle — that is what Daddy thinks, gotta have an angle, an argument, why not reduce it all, I should be able to score off this as long as I don't mind using my early trauma, my dead mother as collateral, hey, why not, she's not going to care, right? Why not spend these little pieces of memory. Why not sell them to the highest offer?

MEMORY HOUSE
Kathleen Tolan

Dramatic
Maggie, forties

*Maggie is talking to her teenaged daughter Katia, whom she and
her husband adopted when she was nine years old.*

MAGGIE: At night I'd tuck you in, and you would say, "Talk story." Do
you remember? When you came here, all the tests, doctors, therapy
and support groups, the list from the doctor of possible "complica-
tions," prenatal, postnatal, genetic, poor medical or nutritional care,
the possible traumas, many things, the one that got me was the potential . . . "failure to thrive." Once, I heard you, in the night, I rushed
to your bed, you were sitting up, frozen, eyes wild, I said, what?
    You said, "Mr. McGregor." . . . I realized you were dreaming
about Peter Rabbit. I wasn't sure whether to feel terrible that I'd read
you something so terrifying, or relieved, that you had arrived. You
were here . . . Your first day here I gave you oatmeal. You wouldn't
eat it. Then I boiled an egg and you ate it and I boiled you another
and another. You ate twelve eggs that day and then got sick and I
put you to bed and wondered, how is it I thought I could be a
mother?
    Do you remember Rice Krispies?
    How much you liked them and I said yes, snap crackle and pop,
I loved that too when I was a kid. And then you decided they were
too loud, they hurt your ears. So I bought earplugs and taped them
to the box of Rice Krispies. And each day at breakfast you would
very solemnly pour out the Rice Krispies, put in your earplugs, pour
the milk and eat them up.
    And when you were in *Alice in Wonderland*, you were such a nice
eaglet. . . .

Yes. And at some point Alice says "Let me try to remember the things I used to know." I wrote it down on a scrap of paper in the dark of the theater, still have the paper, the handwriting all skewed . . . It seemed like the most beautiful sentence I'd ever heard. "Let me try to remember the things I used to know." . . . The sound of it, the cadence, and the . . . whimsy or something, the melancholy, the yearning, how familiar I guess, the wish, and the impossibility of actually remembering what you used to know, and . . . and you, those early years, not knowing, not knowing what happened to you, to your mother, thinking about your mother so much, what happened, what happened to her, and did I do everything I could to know, to be sure . . .

When we brought you here, they said the transition needed to be slow. I made your room very spare. One day I walked into your empty room and . . . began to cry . . . and then I thought, don't do this, don't get attached to the idea of her, of what should be. And I looked up and you were standing there. You looked so guarded, so lost, and I thought, this is something I will do, I will serve this child.

And then all of that turned out to be meaningless. Or, maybe not meaningless. But it fades in the light of . . .

Of . . . of the love. . . .

I fell in love with you.

MESSAGE FROM THE DRIVER

Katie Bull

Dramatic

Woman, late thirties. A working-mom, jazz singer, and teacher . . . She has the "look" they now call East Village Bohemian, which she got before it was a look — (long, loose hair, a knee length colorful sweater worn with a mix of fabrics from different cultures) — and which she now wears unintentionally. She has a journalistic impulse to engage in questioning dialogue.

Setting: October of 2001, New York City. Based on a true story. A Woman is coming home from a performance in the East Village of Manhattan at around 11:00 P.M. She hails a taxi, and goes for a ride she didn't expect. Suffering from post 9/11 stress, she is profoundly startled by a fire she witnesses as they are driving, thinking it might be a bomb. They drive on, and the taxi driver, a Pakistani man, engages her in a dialogue about 9/11. At one point he tells her he knows "where the bombs are" and that his father is in the Pakistani CIA. She asks to get out of the cab, but he suggests that they are "OK." The ride home becomes an inner transport between two different people, from different cultures, into greater intimacy — perhaps. Can we ever really know who we are with? In their conversation he asks her where she was on September 11th. The following monologue is her response to his question.

WOMAN: *(Feigned control, fast and nervous, she answers to demonstrate she is not afraid.)* I was at home, my husband took the kids to school that morning. I sat and did some work. I was writing a syllabus for my students, updating it, for the university. I didn't even know it was happening. *(Woman looks out the window — her rhythm shifts as her memory pulls her into imagery. She is alternately talking directly to*

Driver, then drawn back into the images of that day — looking toward the front window or the side window of the taxi, following the images. Acknowledging his presence, drifting back and forth between past and present.) My husband called me. He just said, two planes hit the World Trade Center, they think it's terrorism. Stay where you are, I've got the kids. They were at school. But the school is on 13th Street. So they were really downtown, and the subways were shut down. God, it was so scary. *(Pause.)* We didn't know what was coming next. *(Pause.)* I went to the TV, and there it was. The first tower, black smoke billowing. And I knew it would fall right then and there. And then the doorbell rang. It was the phone guy. *(Laughs at the absurdity.)* There to fix the second jack. And I just looked at him, he had a friend with him, this woman. And we all just said, oh my God. And we all stood and watched TV. And I said, it's going to fall. And he said, no way. And I said, yes it is. And then it did. And he said, no way, again. He said, it's like a movie, and I said, God, it's not a movie. And I talked to my husband again, before the satellites went down — he was at this friend of ours' house, a mother and father of one of my daughter's classmates. The father is a former fireman. He has a construction company now. He was already going down there. He lived. He injured himself. But the satellites went down. I didn't know what was happening. But they came home later when the train lines went back up. I have never hugged like that. Never been so grateful. *(Silence. Woman is nearly overwhelmed by the memory. Then her focus shifts and she looks at him quite intently. Silence.)*

(Cautiously.) And you? Where were you?

THE MOONLIGHT ROOM
Tristine Skyler

Dramatic
Sal, sixteen

Sal is sitting in a hospital emergency room along with Joshua. They are waiting for news of the fate of a friend.

SAL: *(Not angry at him, but sad, confiding her frustration to him.)* What do you know? Your mom's with someone. She's happy. My mom barely goes out. She says she'd rather stay home and clean the apartment. I'm not even allowed to have friends over because they'll interfere with her depression. And she doesn't want to wash her hair. Sometimes she goes a whole week. I tell her that if maybe we had people around she would start to feel better. But she doesn't listen. She'll sit there watching *Jeopardy* and bad-mouth my dad. The same speech I've been hearing since he left. On and on and on and on. And then when he comes over to pick me up, she puts on lipstick! She doesn't wash her hair, and she has on the same outfit she's worn for three days, but she puts on lipstick! I swear one night I'm going to go out, and I'm just not going to come home. *(They sit in silence for a few beats. Sal becomes embarrassed.)* I just don't want to have to call her. *(Pause.)* You don't realize how lucky you are. You do whatever you want. You could come home tomorrow and it's fine. I come home tomorrow and I'm on the back of a milk carton.

THE MOONLIGHT ROOM
Tristine Skyler

Dramatic
Sal, sixteen

Sal is waiting in a hospital emergency room for news of the fate of a friend. Here, she is talking to her mother.

SAL: *(Reluctantly.)* I got lost. . . .
    When I left Josh's house. . . .
    (Disoriented, full of adrenaline and confusion and fear.) . . . I was going to take the C at 103rd and then get the crosstown. So I walked out of their building and I went to their corner, and the cars seemed to be going uptown, so I assumed it was Amsterdam and I just kept walking. I didn't look at the sign. But then all of a sudden I couldn't remember which way his street went. I didn't know which way I was heading. Was I walking towards Broadway or Columbus? And then, I don't know what happened, suddenly everything started to look unfamiliar. There was a supermarket at the next corner that I'd never seen before. A big Pathmark. And people were coming in and out. And I thought about asking someone for directions but then nobody in that neighborhood ever really looks like they know where they're going either. So I kept going up the street and I remember knowing that I should have passed Broadway by then. And when I crossed the street, I could see the moon reflecting off the water through the trees across the street, and I realized I had walked all the way to Riverside. But the weird thing was, I didn't turn around. I walked up to somebody's front steps instead and sat down because I was too tired to go back. Really lethargic, like I just couldn't take another step. So I sat there for a while, and I could see someone watching television through a window across the street and I just kept staring. Staring at how beautiful it was, the way the television looked in the dark, the way the light kept moving. And after a while, I don't

know how long, a woman walked up to the building with her dog and started talking to me. She said there'd been an accident a few blocks down with tons of police, and that if I was going to be walking around I should be careful. That there had been a bad accident and that whenever there's an emergency, the streets are a little worse in the surrounding areas because all the criminals feel like temporarily the heat is off. Like the cops are busy on 97th Street so I don't have to worry if I just rob someone at gunpoint on 105th, like a built-in diversionary tactic, that sort of thing. But it took this woman about twenty minutes to tell me all this, because half her conversation was directed at me and half at her dog. As if he was going to contribute to the conversation. So finally I got up and left. I took another street and went to the subway. And all that time I'd been walking around, I never heard any sirens . . . *(Sal stops, she looks at her mother.)*

MOOT THE MESSENGER
Kia Corthron

Dramatic
Mary Pat, late teens, early twenties

Mary Pat is a U.S. soldier, in prison for Iraqi prisoner abuse. Here, she is talking to a journalist who is the central character in the play.

MARY PAT: Well they called me and they said there'd been an attempted escape and these prisoners done it and they was stompin' on their hands, and first thing I thought was Wow! MI is tough! Later they hit a prisoner so hard knocked him out, and I thought Huh. That didn't seem necessary, and they ordered Push this man into the pile! And I did, they was *clothed,* they was fully dressed at this point so I done what they said, pushed him, my orders, and then I could see things was startin' to get a little haywire and my stomach was startin' to feel kinda funny, and what I did, what I did next totally under orders that was the major problem was I took a picture. I never seen a nekked man before MI interrogations I swear! And I just about turned beet red first time I did. But they said Take the picture and I help up the camera and I snapped, and later that day I felt sick, and what I really shoulda done was report it, and I got a year for the picture and not reportin' it, and this is somethin' I repeated a lot in court so not to keep beatin' a dead horse but Military Intelligence was right there seein' instructin' and sanctionin' and if I *had* reported it and government'd been in a different mood I might be here anyway, disobeyin' and defyin' a superior so I guess there's no point in keep goin' over it in my head, what I coulda done different what I shoulda done different. . . .

(Pause.) I feel bad. Sometimes I get depressed, year in the brig, but most days I try to be up, coulda been a lot longer. Which is what the Iraqis wanted, and which maybe I deserve, which then gets me down again. I regret it happened, but what I shoulda done

instead . . . rack my brain and just don't quite know what that mighta been. I hear a lot of "remorse," "mistaken judgment" but the people utterin' it never seem to suggest my mistaken judgment was joinin' the reserves in the first place. Hindsight 'course wish I'd just gone on and blowed the whistle, though I hear a guy that did is suddenly the most unpopular person in his home town. I coulda told MI to fuck off, not that it woulda stopped 'em, I don't know what I coulda done to stop 'em in the moment besides pray they stopped themselves. Which I did.

MOOT THE MESSENGER
Kia Corthron

Dramatic
Louise, late teens, early twenties

> *Louise, like her friend Mary Pat, is being tried for abusing Iraqi*
> *prisoners while serving at that infamous prison in Iraq. She is ex-*
> *plaining what went down to the American journalist who is the cen-*
> *tral character in this play.*

LOUISE: OK well like how's somebody trained as a mechanic suddenly
s'posed to be a prison guard? *(Briar starts writing.)* And like the one
person who *was* a guard back home says *he* didn't even feel trained,
he knew about American convicted felons he knew nothin' 'bout
POWs or civilian detained, that don't even take into account we don't
speak the same language, totally different culture, and some a this
stuff maybe we're just s'posed to learn on the job but *all* of it? And
there's thousands a them, nine hundred on our watch alone, and *seven
a us.* And all the attention on Abu Ghraib well you go snoopin'
around betchu find the other facilities ain't s' up to par neither. And
we've been like totally on our own, like sometimes the battalion commander would override the company commander's command, mixed
signals half the time just tryin' to figure it out ourself. And we don't
know what we're doin! and basic taught Don't question an order's
morality just do it! Ask your brother. So at least when MI gave an
order it was clear and I ain't sayin' what MI said was right, I'm just
sayin' — That girl that got in the big trouble? She's a pfc! How in
the hell's world think a private first class just took over and went
wild with nobody above givin' her the wink wink to do it? . . .
    Bush wanted to tear this place down, this ugly stain on the new-
born nation, but the Iraqis said Forget it: crime scene. How come
he didn't tear it down before? All that blood from Saddam's torture
and executions, didn't seem that he cared s'much about the bad

memories before the bad press came out. *(Turns to Briar, tears:)* Do I sound guilty? I'm not I didn't do anything! But sometimes . . . Sometimes I'm scared I'd been in the wrong place wrong time . . . They kept tellin' us it was important. They kept sayin' "Soften up the prisoners, Soften 'em up," said we were helpin' the CIA nab Al Qaeda, people home'd think we're heroes! . . .

I never even hearda no Geneva Conventions 'til recently, my friend Mary Pat claims one day somebody mentioned 'em, like maybe a three-minute lecture which obviously I didn't retain. First I remember hearin' 'bout 'em was when the President goes they don't apply to us so at that point it seemed kinda silly to find out what the heck they were. "Soften up the prisoners, Soften up the prisoners Al Qaeda" and at the time we were gettin' hit hard, mortars and missiles, see that big hole out front? Fallujah ain't far from here! And everybody hatin' us and no one properly supervisin' us, we shoulda been home! We shouldn'ta never been here!

MOOT THE MESSENGER
Kia Corthron

Dramatic
Briar, twenties to thirties

Briar is an American journalist covering the war in Iraq. She is talking to a fellow journalist, Hamid, who works for al-Jazeera.

BRIAR: I'm embedded with these soldiers. Three men and a woman, though it feels weird to say that cuz their faces all looked sixteen, and they were really nice, one looked a lot like my brother. And they were really nice, and nobody said this exactly but it was really clear they expected I would write nice things, like what they were doing was right, of course they'd want that, who'd want it reported this is all bullshit? Which translated another way is they're risking their lives cuz they're all fools. So sometimes saying the truth I felt a little like I was betraying them and one day, recently, it got scary, *really* scary and with the bombing all around one of 'em told me Take this grenade in case they were all killed and I didn't want to, journalists are neutral observers and by picking up a weapon we become combatants, though I gotta admit a slight twinge of excitement in just being part of it, how far we've come since Panama and Granada! And the secret is this has always been my dream: war correspondent. Telling the public the truth, I've seen old Vietnam news footage I could do that! But Vietnam journalists were a complete separate entity from the troops, no confusion, and if the adversarial forces start seeing journalists as armed opponents, participants, then we're all in trouble, though sad to say there's plenty of press out there who offered *no* resistance to the idea of joining in the fight look at me! We eat with them sleep with them *dress* like them, the other side *could* mistake us for them but more important *we* could mistake us for them. So after our particularly frightening episode, and seeing the soldiers I'd been with for weeks shaking and desperately trying to remember all they learned and how it applies here, and desperately trying not to cry for their mamas, and that day reporting back I said three words I swore I'd never utter, I wasn't gonna be like the other so-called journalists here I'd stay professional, neutral, and then they flew out of my mouth: "Us." "Them." "Enemy." And even with my shame I can't stop feeling those words, and I wanted to call my boss to say I have to come home I'm losing my objectivity and the only reason I didn't was because I was pretty sure his reply would be "Get it back." But things have calmed since, and I got a call saying I could leave if I want and I said "I want."

OCTOPHOBIA
James Still

Dramatic
Skater, a young woman

A young woman talks to us about her passion for skating.

SKATER: I'm skating. I FEEL myself, SEE myself, I HEAR myself skating. I hear my past, I hear my heartbeat, I hear God — laughing. I think that he's laughing because skating around and around on frozen water is something he never imagined we would invent. I just don't think he thought it through far enough. Maybe we've been around too long if it's come down to ice skating. God made roses. Man made skating.

(*Beat.*)

My dad says that roses have been growing on this planet for over thirty-five million years. That sounds like a long time. I was skating when I thought about THIS for the first time: that dinosaurs couldn't survive, but roses did. I bet God just shakes his head about that one.

I'm skating. I'm thinking about a moment when I was eight years old . . . It's snowing, it's Los Angeles. I'm in the backyard, wearing a one-piece bathing suit surrounded by my father's roses which he loves more than he loves my mom. When he calls his roses "Hybrid Perpetuals" — it sounds like he's making a wish. I hold a rose against each ear like — ear muffs . . . Like hearing the sounds of the ocean in seashells, the roses turn the sounds of my parents fighting into . . . Romance.

I'm skating. The other little girls would cry when they fell on the ice. I would just lie there, listening to the frozen water moving under my weight. It sounded like God — singing. And I started to sing along. This coach watched me skate and fall and sing with God — and she thought it was poetry. I thought it was heaven.

Skating early in the mornings, when it's still dark, with no one sitting in the stands but your dreams and fears — THAT'S poetry. I don't dream when I sleep. I dream when I skate. This one dream that I have is about me, I'm running from something — a dinosaur, a judge, a TV camera — and I'll realize I'm running — not in circles. I'm running in figure-eights. It's the only shape I know by instinct . . . I stop running from the dinosaur and start running in a figure-eight AWAY from the figure-eight and so I never get away. Pushing off one foot to another, making these big sweeping turns, tracing a giant "eight" in the ice — I feel like I'm crawling along the outside of my grandmother's hips. Or I'm stuck to the lips of that man who always stares at me. An oval-shaped table — family dinners where the food kind of all mushes together and makes this quilt of smells that makes me want to throw up. When I get that look in my eyes, my coach calls it nerves, that I'm nervous, that it's just butterflies. And when she says this, I open my mouth to deny it and all of these butterflies spill out of my mouth and fly around my head in little figure-eights. And then I spend the next four-and-a-half minutes chasing butterflies across the ice. . . Running away from butterflies, jumping/turning/leaping/spinning — turning my fear of figure-eights into something beautiful, heartbeat by heartbeat, like a rose in the snow, like a wish, like romance. I'm skating — *(Gasping for breath, whispers:)* I can hardly breathe.

THE OUTRAGEOUS ADVENTURES OF SHELDON & MRS. LEVINE

Sam Bobrick and Julie Stein

Comic
Mrs. Levine, forties to fifties

This is an epistolary play consisting entirely of letters exchanged between a Jewish mother and her wayward son. Sheldon has called his mother a lunatic. Here, she is replying.

MRS. LEVINE: *(Softly.)* Lunatic! Lunatic! *(She takes a deep breath. Her anger builds.)* Well, Sheldon, maybe I am a lunatic. Maybe you have to be to survive in today's world. How sane do you really want to be knowing we live in a world where the ice caps are melting, the ozone layer is disintegrating and the banks don't give away free toasters anymore? How much stability is healthy when we know we have to live with dirty air, acid rain and fruit that rots in your grocery bag before you get home? Doesn't it bother you, my dear son, that the meat they sell us is so full of steroids, the cows could play basketball for the Knicks? Doesn't it burn your ass, dear Sheldon, that those sleaze-ball politicians we elect to take care of us, all have better retirement and medical plans than we do? And all this new technology that's supposed to make life better doesn't do anything except give me a headache. Download, interface, Web sites, search engines, A-O-L, I-P-O, and that W-W-Dot Com Shit. And the noise. The constant noise that goes on and on and never stops. Beepers beeping, car alarms screaming, cell phones ringing, in the streets, on the trains, in my head. Just how good is that for one's mental well being? And everywhere you go people giving you the finger. My landlord, my paperboy and that nun I sometimes sit next to on the bus . . . You want to know why? Because the world is full of people wound so tight that any minute they can snap like a pretzel. Sanity, Sheldon? Why? What's the point? Let me tell you kiddo, if one morning you wake up and you're not a lunatic, there's something seriously wrong with you. *(A beat.)* Dear Sheldon. It's been weeks since I've heard from you. Was it something I said? *(A beat.)* It's been several months and still no word from you. Even the mailman is starting to ask questions. *(A beat.)* Sheldon Levine. My last letter sent to Yuma was returned to me. I've gone to the police but they're so busy trying to stay out of jail themselves that until you're missing for at least five years they don't want to be bothered. So I'm taking matters into my own hands. I'm putting your picture on a milk carton. I'm paying extra for chocolate. *(A beat.)* Dear Sheldon. It's now been six months since I've heard from you, so if you decide to come home and if I'm not here, check the hospitals. If I'm not there, check the cemeteries.

PASSIVE BELLIGERENCE
Stephen Belber

Comic
Gail, twenties to thirties

Gail, a well-dressed young woman, is interviewing two men, Dan and Jeff, for a most important job: Gail's boyfriend.

GAIL: Good, good. *(Putting resumé down, addressing them both:)* Well as I said, I'm a little pressed for time today. I told myself that I would hire someone by — *(Looking at watch.)* — five o'clock, and here it is, five o'clock, I think I've interviewed sixty people already and I still can't seem to find someone I like. But you're both pleasant surprises and both very qualified so I feel like I'm almost there. So, thanks for that.

As you can probably imagine, when I asked myself what the qualities were that I was looking for in a full-time lover, a number of variables presented themselves to me. To begin with, availability. My husband and I have only been married a year but he's already begun avoiding his corporeal responsibility to me. Maybe he's got someone else, power to him if he does, all I know is that he's putting in 65-hour weeks down there at Paine Webber which really doesn't leave him with the time and energy required to properly service his wife. And the fact is, this little car needs more than the occasional tune-up.

Secondly, I need imagination. For all of the indubitably imaginative financial flourishes that Jim whips out as he climbs the corporate ladder, the man has nary whipped out a ball of twine thus far with his wife, to say nothing of ankle chains or the occasional prison warden routine. And so I seek creativity. And let us not forget adventurism, foresight and, of course, foreplay, although I'm not one of these women who get carried away with the conceit. My philosophy since the eighth grade has been: Put the sausage in the oven while the coal's still hot, and stoke, for God's sake, stoke, stoke!

And yet, thirdly, I need someone who challenges me, not just sexually — although mostly sexually — but also emotionally and intellectually. Jim's good with numbers but the man couldn't write a poem to save his life, much less recite *The Wasteland* while mounting me from behind. You can both take note of that.

So I think that essentially what I'm looking for is a well-endowed man — and please don't interpret that in a merely juvenile way, for I mean well-endowed in every sense of the phrase, most notably in terms of integrity. *(To Dan:)* I like a man who can sit here and tell me that he's into passivity; *(To Jeff:)* or a man who's not afraid to admit that he has a violent streak, especially when he has no idea that it's a perfect qualification for the job he's just applied for. So that's nice, but I still have one very important question I'd like to put forth to you gentlemen: Why do you think you should have this job?

THE PENETRATION PLAY
Winter Miller

Dramatic
Rain, twenties

Rain is confessing her love to her best friend Ash, another woman.

RAIN: Last night wasn't some drunk groping thing where one thing led
to another — what I said last night, about you — my point is —
anyway, my point is that the way I am around you is completely different from the way I've felt around anybody else. There are real feel-
ings there — . . .

Let me finish. I've been playing this over in my head for hours
and it has to come out now. So just — let me say it. . . .

I know you as well as I know myself — I know you like a scrap-
book, each memory is all stacked up and catalogued — and I trust
you, and trust in you and I — I was always afraid to cross the line
with us, in case it didn't live up to my expectations — but it — you,
us . . . felt right. I mean innately right. The way our bodies fit together — that doesn't just come out of nowhere — with women,
the maneuvering part, getting your bodies in just the right place —
it's harder — but last night, it was so natural, everything clicked into
place . . . You felt it — it's the most intimate two people can be —
the place where the physical collides with the emotional and — I
felt this urge to weep. But I was afraid. Afraid of nearly everything,
how much I wanted you, wanted you to last. And I held you and I
said I loved you . . . and you didn't — or you couldn't say it back. . . .

I'm not done. You said — do you know what came out of your
mouth — you said "this night is so over the top — Rich thinks he's
in love with me." . . .

I think that was the exact moment I felt my heart break. Seriously. You don't think you can feel that sort of thing — like women
who say they felt the instant of conception — but you can feel it —

THE PENETRATION PLAY
Winter Miller

Dramatic
Rain, twenties

Rain is confessing her love to her best friend Ash, another woman.

RAIN: Why is it I'm so easy for every other girl but you to fall in love with. They're not necessarily straight, maybe they could be something else in different circumstances — but they fall in love with me and they don't even see it coming. They're blown away by how easy it is to be with a woman — the friendship part and the sex is so good because nobody's ever listened to them like that — they swear they don't even miss a man's body. Before they know it, they've given over. The reason: Because they know somewhere, it will never last, that it has an expiration date because they're not going to spend the rest of their lives with another woman — it doesn't fit into their wedding fantasy or their nuclear family — so they fall in love, because they're caught completely unawares by the potential of it ever working out — ever lasting — but after a few months or years of this — they get it. They see their friends getting married, living the dream, and they hear a nagging voice inside grow louder and louder until it's screaming END IT, you can't go on. So they do. And they cry and they swear they don't know what's happening and it isn't you and they haven't even fallen out of love with you — but it's over. Because they've decided it's the end of the line. A year or so later, some mutual friend lets slip they're going to her wedding . . . and you become, a moment in time. An interesting sidebar — a piece of trivia for her new friends and her inner circle. You become a reference, proof of tolerance, or in some cases, of a wild streak — a status symbol of having dared . . .
Fuck it. Fuck 'em all. Marry Rich.

RED DEATH
Lisa D'Amour

Dramatic
Connie, twenties to thirties

Connie is speaking to her husband, Prospero Albright, aboard their yacht. Earlier in the scene, Connie realized that Jane Withers, the woman who had murdered their daughter and burned down their house, had been living on their boat for weeks, in disguise. This causes her to faint. While she's passed out, Prospero and Jane discuss the situation. During their conversation, Connie wakes up. Here she speaks to herself, to Jane and to Prospero.

CONNIE: I see the green grass round Grass Lake. And then I am in my hometown and there is the bicycle my father bought me when I was five years old, and the knee I skinned learning to ride it. And hello there I am junior prom queen! This is the way one sips a drink, this is the way one waves good-bye. Boo hoo my reign is over! Anyway it's almost just as good, sitting alone in my room making paper cutouts of the girl I wish I was. The hips are adequate but it's what is inside that counts: that extraordinary flame in the center of my ribs. The bus toward California is moldy and crowded, but I must get away: I am making my way in the world. Anyway one day I will have my own girl. I am making rice I am making yellow squash I am selling my first house I am making peas. And when he is down on one knee before me there is a flash and I am back inside the oval of my baby bassinet. I am a baby and everything is light, my eyes are wide and through the primary colors of the mobile I see a woman crying hard and she reaches toward me with the handful of powder and pat pat pats my belly and it feels exquisite but her tears won't stop they drop drop drop on my soft skin. And then I realize, this is it —

SCHOOLGIRL FIGURE
Wendy MacLeod

Seriocomic
Renee, seventeen, now the reigning anorexic

> *Her best friend Patty, her rival anorexic Jeanine and the prize, The
> Bradley, have just abandoned her to go eat, thus ending the Car-
> penter's competition to be Queen. Renee decides to stay the course
> despite what everybody else decides.*

RENEE: No great loss. Patty will be happier in the Midwest — parkas cam-
ouflage a multitude of sins. And as for The Bradley, he wasn't really
the prize, he was just the tacky little statuette; the gas station glasses,
the stuffed bear at the fair! The prize is actually . . . well, true story.
Back in the days when I had muscles, I would rent a patch of ice
every morning before it was light and go out there and try to mas-
ter my school figures. I would fiercely skate that figure eight, because
down the pike the school figures would count for 50 percent of my
Olympic score. I practiced them even when I was on land, waiting
in line for the water fountain, pressing my sneakers into imaginary
blades. I spent the wee hours of my pre-pubescence obsessed with
the Russian judge's good opinion of my outside edge and do you
know what happened? They did away with the school figure part of
the competition. Just did away with it. Because nobody saw them.
Nobody *wanted* to see them. The audience just cared about the part
where the skinny girl wears a skimpy leotard trimmed with marabou
and jumps around to the disco version of *Carmen*. What can we learn
from this? I'm sorry . . . I forgot what I was going to say. Is it cold
in here or is it just me? Oh, I know. What we have learned is that
there is only so much in this world that we can control so by all means
let us control what we can, achieve what we must. Perfection.

> *(When she speaks in rhyme we realize she's imagining herself in The
> Pantheon of dead girls.)*

If you're happy with who you are
It's clearly time to raise the bar
Now it's time for my good-byeses
To you poor girls of the larger sizes

SECOND
Neil Utterback

Dramatic
Vick, thirties

Vick is a tough, no-nonsense reporter. She is talking to a woman named Lauren. This is the second half of a much longer monologue.

VICK: Who is this? This could be anyone. This could be my accountant brother in Connecticut. But they all claim they have seen a miracle. Maybe, maybe even, the Messiah. Amazing, you say? No. It's ridiculous. I mean, if you ask me, the real miracle is getting twenty-two New Yorkers to believe such a preposterous thing. And he can't be found. No one is coming forward — or rather everyone is coming forward saying they are sure their neighbor is the "Miracle Man," or "Saint Nicholas," or "Captain Christmas" if you work for the *Post*. But you know what it is? It's Prescott, that prick. He's afraid of me. He's afraid and he's determined to sabotage my career and my credibility and take me out of the running for his job, which I am in. So, on some level I have to respect that fat, sweaty troll bastard. But that smarmy creep has a second thing coming, believe you me. I will get his job and run him out of the business and the tri-state area. *(She goes to get a glass and returns.)* And then there's this Armageddon blizzard. You're lucky your plane even made it in. Another hour and no way, baby. Henry is calling for it to be the worst storm in *recorded history.* Of course, Henry doesn't know the first thing about the weather. They only keep him on because he's older than Moses. Prescott, as God is my witness, he's actually moist. His skin has this . . . it's like his parents hawked up a loogie and christened it. *(She pours a glass of wine.)* Oh, *and,* of the twenty-two people who stuck around and gave their names, half of them are hookers, drug addicts, or criminals themselves. These are my sources? They're no help. I tried interviewing one guy, who I tracked, I swear to God, into an abandoned warehouse. He couldn't get through an entire sentence without having some kind of *(Vick begins jerking in spasms.)* fit.

SECOND
Neil Utterback

Dramatic
Lauren, thirties

Lauren is talking to Vick, a tough, no-nonsense reporter.

LAUREN: *(Pause.)* I want to hope for the beautiful and the seemingly impossible. Did you know I started playing the lottery? Me. I need to believe that improbable things can happen. So, I play the lottery, building faith. And what is faith really but a commitment to hope. It's hope without the logical affliction of worry. One simply has to let go and say, "I choose to believe — between hope and worry — I choose hope." And if you can do that — that's faith. Or love, which is really the same thing, faith and love. In fact, love, in and of itself, doesn't exist. What we know, or think we know of love, is an amalgam of trust, or faith, and lust. To say "I love you" has little or no impact. To say, "I trust you" which is to say, "I have faith in you," is a far greater proclamation. If you asked anyone on the street, "Whom do you love?" — they could probably rattle off a dozen names. Ask him, "Whom do you *trust?*" — most people are lucky if they could name one. Lust is easy. *You* lust for virtually every other woman you see in the city. But trust? Faith?

SQUATS
Martin Jones

Dramatic
Cece, sixteen

Cece is a homeless teenager. Here, she is in a motel room with a man named Tucker.

CECE: *(Sighs, heavily.)* Well, I set my first [fire] when I was about nine or ten. The summer my old man left us. Me and Bobby Conroy . . . we were playin' in his daddy's old milk barn. This was when we still lived up at Rumford. Anyway, we were punchin' holes in the barn wall with a ball-peen hammer. Bobby found a can of paint thinner in the tack room. And I supplied the matches. Went up like the Fourth of July. All the neighborin' farmers stood on the hill, watchin' it burn all night long. I was scared, so I was hidin' behind my mama's legs, but I'd peek out from time to time from behind her dress. She was cryin'. I think she knew. She squeezed my hand so hard I got a big bruise, but I didn't care. I couldn't take my eyes offa those colors reachin' up to that black sky — all sorta Christmas red and Florida orange. Bobby Conroy finally broke down and confessed. Got his ass whipped good. I never told. Mama didn't say nothin', but I could tell she knew. *(Pause.)* Couple years later, she'd be at work at the paper mill — be gone all day — and I'd be home alone or in school — always thinkin' about those colors. Couldn't get 'em outta my head. That summer, I sorta went wild. I burnt three barns, an old fishin' boat, and a couple of abandoned house trailers. Then I got caught. . . .

You think that's funny? . . .

I never did it to hurt people. Just like to watch things burn. I set some brush fires too. Some guy showed me how. He'd catch a big, ol' jack rabbit in a snare, then he'd hold the rabbit by his ears, and dunk his hindquarters in a bucket of kerosene. Light the tail, and set him loose. A jackrabbit will zig-zag two or three miles 'fore he realizes he's dead. I didn't do much of that, 'cause I didn't like the idea of killin' anything, even if it was a pesty rabbit.

SELF DEFENSE; OR, DEATH OF SOME SALESMEN
Carson Kreitzer

Dramatic
Jo, thirties

Jolene Palmer (Jo) is a prostitute on death row for the killing of seven johns.

JO: Now they got their fucking movie coming out, and I haven't even been convicted yet. That's *gotta* be illegal. I swear.

"First Female Serial Killer." And I haven't even been convicted yet. I'm right in the middle of this shit.

An' they got me bein' played by SOMEBODY I NEVER EVEN HEARD OF. They coulda at least got Jodie Foster or something. I know I . . . ain't that Pretty, but they could rough her up some.

We know she can play a hooker. She was real good in that *Taxi Driver*. Actually, I looked . . . well, I looked a lot like her when that movie came out. Don't look nothing like her now. Maybe I would, if I got to go home after shooting, instead a . . . 'Course, at that time home was a car out in the woods. Fuckin' . . . *freezing*. I was cold all my life, Florida always sounded like a good deal.

Anyway, we know she can play a hooker, we know she can get raped. How about coming full circle and we see her packin' a little Justice? Huh? Now there's a movie I'd pay money to see.

Not some fuckin' bullshit lyin-ass TV crap fuckin' Marg Helgenberger fuckin' Alyssa Milano. Who the fuck are these people?

SPEAKING WELL OF THE DEAD

Israel Horovitz

Dramatic
Willa, twenty

Willa's father was killed in the World Trade Center attack. This is direct address to the audience.

WILLA: There was this tall skinny guy who got killed at the World Trade Center, along with my father. They worked in the same department, together. Currency traders. This guy had this little son — Alex — also tall and skinny. The father and Alex were really really close. I remember my father saying that Alex and his father has started playing golf together on Staten Island, and that Alex was this really amazing golfer for his age. Alex must only be about, I dunno, 8 or 9, *now.* No more than that. Really cute sweet kid. After the Towers came down, my mother told me this amazing story about Alex trying to get phone calls through to Heaven, to talk to his father. He would argue with operators, supervisors, whoever would listen. He was getting really upset, so, finally, Alex comes up with this new idea, to write notes to his father, put them in balloons, and, like, float them up to Heaven. The mother doesn't have the heart to tell him the truth, so, she goes along with it, and now, every day, Alex writes these little notes, and he and his mother take them to this party store on the corner of West 10th Street and Greenwich Ave., and for 25 cents, apiece, this really nice shop-guy in a turban puts Alex's notes in these balloons, which he fills with helium, and Alex and his mom take them outside and let them go, watch them fly up to Heaven. *(Beat.)* Alex is still waiting for his dad to answer him. *(Beat.)* They never found my dad's body. That makes it so totally harder for my mom to accept his death . . . that it, like, really *happened.* She goes out on our balcony, two or three times a day, and talks to him . . . to my father.

She speaks slowly and clearly, like her words are gonna' float up to him, like the kid's balloons. *(Beat.)* My mom's still waiting for an answer, too. *(Beat.)* I go to college, upstate, in Ithaca. I'm a classics major. Ithaca is named for the second smallest of the seven Ionian Islands in Greece. Ithaca was the home of the Greek hero-king Odysseus. Odysseus cheats on his wife, for years and years. He claims to be away, working, but, in fact, he's out there, sleeping around with nymphs. He fathers an illegitimate son with a witch named Circe. Years later, this bastard son, Telegonus, goes to Ithaca in search of Odysseus — his father — who he finds and kills. I feel as if I've come home from Ithaca to kill *my* father. I know he's already dead, but my mother's re-invented him in a way that's so far from the truth, she's made a kind of saint of him. I mean, she's made him out to be so saintly, she'll never be able to stop mourning him. My job is to tell her the truth — what I know and she doesn't. . . . Sometimes, you have to *act* brave before you can *be* brave.

STRING OF PEARLS
Michele Lowe

Seriocomic
Beth, mid to late thirties

> *Beth has been married for several years to a man who does not show much physical interest in her, much to her frustration. At a high school reunion, she meets a woman who makes an unorthodox suggestion, as to something she might try to rekindle the flame of her marriage.*

BETH: We went home that night and I drank three cups of Maxwell House while he read the *Wall Street Journal*. When he finally came upstairs, it was after three — but I was up and pumping on 22 pistons. As soon as he got into bed, I jumped on top of him and said, Ethan Brown — did you really give that girl Beverly from Camp Anawana, a string of pearls?! And suddenly I felt him in between my thighs, get hard like a rock. And I — I started experiencing the most incredible tingling sensation around my chest.

So I said it again:

A string of pearls Ethan, you gave it to her? And now he's so hard, I'm thinking Oh my god, oh my god, oh my god. And he looks right at me, right in my eyes and he whispers — You want a string of pearls?

And I think if talking about it is going to get him this hard, imagine what he's going to be like when he gives it to me.

So I say, OOOh, yes, Ethan. You bad boy, you never gave me a string of pearls. I want a string of pearls, give it to me. Wham! He rolls over, pins me down and rips off my nightgown. His penis is coming out of his pajamas. He throws off his bottoms and pushes me down toward the end of the bed. And the whole time he's saying, You want a string of pearls? You want a string of pearls? And I'm saying, Yes, Ethan, yes, gimme a string of pearls and the next thing I know he puts his penis between my breasts and whispers,

Squeeeeze it.

OH. OK.

So I squeeze my breasts around his penis.

Now, I'm a 34 double A. The only time I ever used a bra was when I was pregnant with Linda.

But something happened that night, I swear to God. I touched my breasts and they'd grown. I had mango breasts, beachy Gauguin breasts, breasts like you see in a Renoir painting or a B movie. I must have been a 40D. Something — something miraculous was happening. He was growing, I was growing, and now he's pumping between my breasts and I'm getting so turned on and he's saying: Yeah, yeah, yeah, oh, baby, oh, oh, oh, uh-hUH, baby, OH OH OHHH!!

And with no warning whatsoever he comes all over my neck. Then he leans over and whispers: "String of pearls."

THE TAXI CABARET
Peter Mills

Seriocomic
Karen, twenty-something

> The Taxi Cabaret *is a musical about twenty-somethings in the big city. Karen is a teacher, hoping that something exciting will soon happen in her life.*

KAREN: *(Bing-bong. Karen runs after a departing subway.)* Wait! Wait! Wait for me . . . *(She stops, seeing it's a lost cause. Then, waving to the train.)* Good-bye, everybody! They never wave back. Every morning I take the subway, and every morning that same train is there, just pulling away as I come running down the stairs. Sometimes I set my alarm for ten minutes earlier, but even then I still just miss it. I don't mind really. Everyone else in this city, it's like they're in such a hurry to get somewhere. Not me — I'm just glad to be here! I mean, this is New York City, people! Nobody else seems as excited about that. Of course, I've only been here six weeks. In a year or so, I might blend right in with all the other faces on the subway. . . . *(She makes a blasé morning face.)* No, I doubt it. I bet it's a whole different story on that earlier train. I imagine everybody's smiling and chatting . . . enjoying the ride. It's all those people you pass on the street and somehow you can tell that they're five minutes ahead of the game. But all the zombie people on my train, they don't realize how lucky they are to be riding the subway. Think of it — you're there zooming through tunnels, underneath this huge metropolis. It's like you're the blood pumping through the arteries of some giant city-beast. I teach first grade at a school down in the Village, and when we were doing the unit on the circulatory system, I asked if I could take my class on a field trip to the subway. The principal didn't think it was such a good idea. *(Pause.)* Ooh — I love that breeze! You feel it on your face, and then you look and you can see the train way off down the track. But you know it's coming . . . *(Getting louder over the sound of the train approaching.)* That's kind of what every day feels like for me. I feel that breeze, and I know that any minute something huge is gonna come whooshing into my life.

TUMOR
Sheila Callaghan

Dramatic
Sarah, early twenties

Sarah has gotten herself knocked up. This is direct address to the audience.

SARAH: Walking around the women's department in Macy's. There are children everywhere, crawling like arachnids, they have more legs than I thought children were supposed to have but I guess you start to notice these things when you've been hijacked. Looking over their sweaty heads for something simple and angora I recall when angora was simple, when the angora gaze was not flecked with knots of unfiltered mess who run for no reason and stick to everything and wail like original sin multiplied by twelve.

I keep my eyes a safe distance above the swarming ick and spot a garment worthy of my once-upon self. I move towards it as smooth as a rollerball pen. Soon I am close enough to attract its static cling. My hand, electric, rises to the rising sweater arm, also electric, and in our dual reaching pose we are an Italian Renaissance masterpiece. But as my fingers splay for the grasp I feel an icy sludge make its way down my left leg.

I hear this: "It's not my fault, the bottom fell out!" And then a small person is galloping away from me towards a larger person. I look. My entire calf from knee to ankle is covered in a seeping red liquid. Pooling into the side of my sneaker is roughly eight ounces of bright red smashed ice. And lying next to my foot is a Slurpie cup with its bottom in shreds.

That night I dream of buckets and buckets of blood gushing from between my legs.

WAVING GOODBYE
Jamie Pachino

Dramatic
Lily Blue, seventeen

> *Lily is talking to Boggy, her boyfriend, about the impact of her mother's artwork. Lily's mother has recently abandoned her and her father.*

LILY: Boggy sometimes I dream my father falls, and I can catch him. I race and I grope until I'm standing right under him, with my arms open wide. But instead his weight crushes me, and nobody survives. Sometimes my father dies because I'm too insignificant to break his fall. *(Enormously hurt:)* This was my favorite thing she ever did. I was ten when I saw it the first time. She had gone off to . . . the Serengeti I think. The month of March is supposed to be, I don't know — she has this thing about light and water and — she'd gone off before, but this time we were pretty sure she wasn't coming back. And he had to go off on a climb. The hot water heater was busted, the mortgage was overdue — again, Pepper our dog — needed an operation, and he had to leave. So he took me to this locker where she kept her early stuff, because he wanted me to know something about her. To understand why she was right, he said, to go away when the world asked her to, because of what the world got back. Not me, not him, just . . . the world. But there aren't so many ways to say that to a ten-year-old, so he took me to see her work. I didn't know anything about Art, but something about the forearms and the hands . . . my father's hands that she had done . . .

He showed me all the work she'd done right after they met, and told me how she ate Hershey bars at 12,000 feet after climbing without any of the right equipment, and how it was a miracle she didn't die right there. He smiled so big when he explained how those first pieces made her name, how her vision of him had made her — who she turned into — even though she had grown past them and wouldn't look at them anymore. Even though they were his favorites, and my favorites, she had to go off hunting new light. They were so incredible, I almost forgave her.

WHAT THE NIGHT IS FOR
Michael Weller

Dramatic
Lindy, forties

> *Lindy has run into an old flame, Adam. She is very unhappy in her*
> *marriage.*

LINDY: I knew the calm was too good to last. There was a time I could fly
level for months at a time without chemicals.
(Roots in her handbag, speaking faster.)
    This launch feels pretty smooth, relative to some I could name,
like the infamous lawn party / when we moved out here to Hugoland.
Before his family met me / well, refused to in fact, cause Hugh
hadn't first run his bride past the Metz Genetic Quality Control Committee. I wanted to rub their noses in chic, Mama Metz and all her
lumbering Country Club Tutons; My legendary Black and White
Party, oh, Adam, you should have seen it; dance band, tent, even the
food; pasta with white sauce and black truffles, god it was swank. Not
even a freak thunderstorm could blunt the high spirits. It flattened
the entire tent, and everyone went racing into the conservatory, but
Unflappable Lindy strode forth chin high into the storm and pro-
ceeded to re-raise the tent. What could they do but follow me laughing into the downpour, tra-la. Only, when I looked up from wrestling
a tent pole, there they were, motionless silhouettes behind the conservatory windows watching me outside in the rain, raving. Tra-la!
(She stops, taking some pills from her handbag.)
    What a way for poor Hugh to learn his vivacious-if-sometimes-
moody young bride and mother of the bicycle babies was "chemically
challenged." *(Off his look.)* Manic depressive. In the bi-polar sense.
(Beat.) He's been very good about it. Considering I never told him.
(Beat.) He wouldn't have married me, you see. *(Jiggling the pill bot-*
tle.) Water?

[*(Adam gets a glass and hands it to her on the bed.)*]

Squeezies, I call them. We have pet names for the meds, all us ladies of the Bi-Polaroid Society, our support group. Zonkers. Hammers. Whatever sends you back to the D.G.N., the old Dull Gray Nothing, sort of like TV with the sound off. Life without the awful peaks and valleys. Alas, no orgasm, either. Which is why, for gala moments — for *you* — heigh-ho, heigh-ho, it's off the pills we go. And the cow flies over the moon, straight into orbit sometimes. Sorry you had to see this.

(She pops pills and drinks some water.)

They'll kick in by tomorrow. Just taking them helps — psychologically.

THE BEARD OF AVON. ©2001, 2005 by Amy Freed. Reprinted by permission of William Morris Agency, Inc. on behalf of the author by special arrangement with Samuel French, Inc., which has published the entire text in an acting edition and which also handles performance rights. Contact: Samuel French, Inc., 45 W. 25th St., New York, NY 10010; 212-206-8990; www.samuelfrench.com. The play is also published by Smith and Kraus in *New Playwrights: The Best Plays of 2004*.

BRIDEWELL. ©2002 by Charles Evered. Reprinted by permission of the Susan Gurman Agency, 865 West End Ave., New York, NY 10025-8403. The entire text is published in the anthology *The Shoreham and Other Plays*. Contact the Gurman Agency for publisher information and performance rights.

CAVEDWELLER (Based on the novel by Dorothy Allison). ©2004 by Kate Moira Ryan. Reprinted by permission of Beth Blickers, Abrams Artists Agency, 275 7th Ave., New York, NY 10001. The entire text has been published in an acting edition by Dramatists Play Service, which also handles performance rights. Contact: Dramatists Play Service, 440 Park Ave. S., New York, NY 10016; 212-683-8960; www.dramatists.com

THE CLEAN HOUSE. ©2003 by Sarah Ruhl. Reprinted by permission of the author, c/o Bret Adams Ltd., 448 W. 44th St., New York, NY 10036. Contact Bret Adams Ltd. for performance rights. The entire text has been published by Smith and Kraus in *New Playwrights: The Best Plays of 2005*.

COBRA NECK. ©2004 by Keith Josef Adkins. Reprinted by permission of Playscripts, Inc., which has published the entire text in *Trepidation Nation* and which also handles performance rights. Contact: Playscripts, Inc., Box 237060, New York, NY 10023; 212-866-NEW-PLAY; www.playscripts.com

COMMON GROUND. ©2004 by Brendon Votipka. Reprinted by permission of Playscripts, Inc., which has published the entire text in an acting edition and which also handles performance rights. Contact: Playscripts, Inc., Box 237060, New York, NY 10023; 212-866-NEW-PLAY; www.playscripts.com

THE CRAZY TIME. ©2001 by Sam Bobrick. Reprinted by permission of the author. The entire text has been published in an acting edition by Samuel French, Inc., which also handles performance rights. Contact: Samuel French, Inc., 45 W. 25th St., New York, NY 10010; 212-206-8990; www.samuelfrench.com

CUTRS! ©2005 by Allison Moore. Reprinted by permission of the author, c/o Maura Teitelbaum, Abrams Artists, 275 7th Ave., New York, NY 10001. The entire text has been published by The New York Theatre Experience, Inc. (www.Newyorktheatreexperience.org) in *Plays and Playwrights 2005*, as part of the anthology play *Honor*. Contact Abrams Artists Agency for performance rights.

DARK RIVER. ©2004 by Alexa Romanes. Reprinted by permission of Samuel French Ltd., 52 Fitzroy St., London W1T 5JR, England, which has published the entire text in an acting edition and which handles performance rights.

DEN OF THIEVES. ©2004 by Stephen Adly Guirgis. Reprinted by permission of John Buzzetti, The Gersh Agency. CAUTION: Professionals and amateurs are hereby warned that *Den of Thieves* is subject to a royalty. It is fully protected under the copyright laws of the United States of America, and of all countries covered by the International Copyright Union (including the Dominion of Canada and the rest of the British Commonwealth), and of all countries covered by the Pan-American Copyright Convention and the Universal Copyright Convention, and of all countries

rights. Contact: Samuel French, Inc., 45 W. 25th St., New York, NY 10010; 212-206-8990; www.samuelfrench.com

KALIGHAT. ©2004 by Paul Knox. Reprinted by permission of the author. The entire text has been published by New York Theatre Experience (www.newyorkexperience.org) in *Plays and Playwrights 2005*. For performance rights, contact the author c/o New York Theatre Experience.

THE LAST DAYS OF JUDAS ISCARIOT. ©2005 by Stephen Adly Guirgis. Reprinted by permission of Farrar, Straus & Giroux, 19 Union Sq. West, New York, NY 10003, which has published the entire text in a trade edition. The entire text has also been published in an acting edition by Dramatists Play Service, which handles performance rights.

THE LEFT HAND SINGING. ©1997, 2004 by Barbara LeBow. Reprinted by permission of Mary Harden, Harden-Curtis Assoc., 850 7th Ave. #903, New York, NY 10019. The entire text has been published in an acting edition by Dramatists Play Service, which also handles performance rights. Contact: Dramatists Play Service, 440 Park Ave. S., New York, NY 10016; 212-683-8960; www.dramatists.com

THE LONG CHRISTMAS RIDE HOME. ©2004 by Paula Vogel. Reprinted by permission of Theatre Communications Group, 520 8th Ave., New York, NY 10018-4156. The entire text has been published in an acting edition by Dramatists Play Service, which also handles performance rights. Contact: Dramatists Play Service, 440 Park Ave. S., New York, NY 10016; 212-683-8960; www.dramatists.com

MEMORY HOUSE. ©2005 by Kathleen Tolan. Reprinted by permission of Peregrine Whittlesey, 279 Central Park W., New York, NY 10024. The entire text has been published by Smith and Kraus in *Humana Festival 2005: The Complete Plays*. For performance rights, contact Peregrine Whittlesey.

MESSAGE FROM THE DRIVER. ©2004 by Katie Bull. Reprinted by permission of the author. The entire text has been published by New York Theatre Experience (www.newyorktheatre experience.org) in *Plays and Playwrights 2005*, as part of *The 29 Questions Project*. Contact the author for performance rights c/o New York Theatre Experience.

THE MOONLIGHT ROOM. ©2004 by Tristine Skyler. Reprinted by permission of Michael Cardonick, Creative Artists Agency, 162 5th Ave., New York, NY 10010. The entire text has been published in an acting edition by Dramatists Play Service, which also handles performance rights. Contact: Dramatists Play Service, 440 Park Ave. S., New York, NY 10016; 212-683-8960; www.dramatists.com

MOOT THE MESSENGER. ©2005 by Kia Corthron. Reprinted by permission of Bret Adams Ltd., 448 W. 44th St., New York, NY 10036. The entire text has been published by Smith and Kraus, Inc. in *Humana Festival 2005: The Complete Plays*. Contact Bret Adams Ltd. for performance rights.

OCTOPHOBIA. ©2004 by James Still. Reprinted by permission of Playscripts, Inc., which has published the entire text in an acting edition and which handles performance rights. Contact: Playscripts, Inc., Box 237060, New York, NY 10023; 212-866-NEW-PLAY; www.playscripts.com

THE OUTRAGEOUS ADVENTURES OF SHELDON & MRS. LEVINE. ©2003 by Sam Bobrick and Julie Stein. Reprinted by permission of the authors. The entire text has been published in an acting edition by Samuel French, Inc., which handles performance rights. Contact: Samuel French, Inc., 45 W. 25th St., New York, NY 10010; 212-206-8990; www.samuelfrench.com

PASSIVE BELLIGERENCE. ©2004 by Stephen Belber. Reprinted by permission of Playscripts, Inc., which has published the entire text in an acting edition and which handles the performance rights. Contact: Playscripts, Inc., Box 237060, New York, NY 10023; 212-866-NEW-PLAY; www.playscripts.com